NEW ENGLAND WALKING ATLAS

NEW ENGLAND WALKING ATLAS

Gary Yanker and Carol Tarlow

McGRAW-HILL PUBLISHING COMPANY

New York   St. Louis   San Francisco   Bogotá
Hamburg   Madrid   Mexico   Milan   Montreal
Paris   São Paulo   Tokyo   Toronto

WALKING WORLD STAFF

Editors: Gary Yanker and Carol Tarlow

Managing Editors: Katherine Burton and David Singleton

Map Illustrator: Barbara Frake

Map Editors: Elina Lowensohn and Susan Henricks

Researchers: Dalia Kandiyoti, Linda Filchev, and Linda Ravin

Business Manager: Kelly C. Kane

1 2 3 4 5 6 7 8 9 FGR FGR 8 9 2 1 0 9

ISBN 0-07-072231-5

LIBRARY OF CONGRESS CATALOGING-IN-PUBLICATION DATA

Yanker, Gary.
    New England walking atlas / Gary Yanker and Carol Tarlow.
        p. cm.
    ISBN 0-07-072231-5
    1. Hiking—New England—Guide-books. 2. Walking—New England—
Guide-books. 3. New England—Description and travel—Guide-books.
I. Tarlow, Carol. II. Title.
GV199.42.C2Y36 1989
917.94—dc19   88-28208
                                                                   CIP

Book design by Sheree Goodman.

Contents

Introduction ix

CONNECTICUT

Eastern Connecticut

1 Rock Spring Wildlife Refuge: Perimeter Trail 1

Western Connecticut

2 Downtown Waterbury 2
3 Kent to Cornwall Bridge: A Walk on
 the Appalachian Trail 5
4 The White Memorial Foundation 7

Northwestern Connecticut

5 Bog Meadow Trail 9

Central Connecticut

6 The Walk, Hartford 11

Southwestern Connecticut

7 Greenwich Point 13
8 Mianus River Gorge: Brink of Gorge Trail 15
9 Sherwood Island Shore Walk 17
10 A Walking Tour of Fairfield 19

South Central Connecticut

11 Willard's Island 21
12 A Walking Tour of Yale 23

Southeastern Connecticut

13 Shoreline Walk in Waterford 26
14 New London: Ocean Beach Park Boardwalk 28
15 Fort Griswold 30
16 A Walking Tour of Norwich 32
17 Stonington Borough 34

MAINE

Southern Maine

18 Kennebunkport 37
19 Portland: Uptown Art Walk 39
20 Old Orchard Beach 41
21 Crescent Beach 43

22 Mackworth Island Nature Walk   44
23 Wolfe's Neck Woods: Shoreline Walk   45
24 Wiscasset Harbor   48
25 Historic Augusta   50
26 Hallowell: Maine's "Antique Capital"   53

Northeastern Maine
27 QuaQuaJo Mountain Nature Walk   55

The Central Coast
28 Bar Harbor Shore Path   57
29 Deer Isle: A Walk in Stonington   59
30 Main Street, Rockland   61

Central Maine
31 Bangor's Historic Districts   63
32 Gulf Hagas   66
33 Mt. Katahdin   67

MASSACHUSETTS

Eastern Massachusetts
34 Boston by Foot: North End Tour   70
35 Boston: Black Heritage Trail   73
36 Old Cambridge Walking Tour   76
37 A Walk along the Charles River   78
38 A Presidential Walk in Brookline   80
39 Breakheart Reservation   82
40 Blue Hills Reservation: Houghton's Pond   84
41 Wellesley College: Alexandra Botanic Garden
    and Hunnewell Arboretum   86
42 Black Pond Preserve   87
43 Hingham Walking Tour   89

Southeastern Massachusetts
44 Plymouth Walking Tour   90
45 Cape Cod: Provincetown Dunes Walk   92
46 Cape Cod Canal   94
47 Cape Cod Rail Trail   96

Western Massachusetts
48 The Mount: Edith Wharton's Home in the
    Berkshires   98
49 Bartholomew's Cobble: Ledges Trail   100
50 Mt. Holyoke and Mt. Norwottuck   102

51 Pike's Pond Trail   104
52 South Taconic Trail and Bash Bish Falls   106
53 Hiking Up Mt. Greylock   108

Central Massachusetts
54 Worcester: God's Acre   110
55 Old Railroad Roadbed Trail   112
56 Mt. Watatic Loop   113

NEW HAMPSHIRE

Eastern New Hampshire
57 Wolfeboro: Three Walks   115

Southeastern New Hampshire
58 Discovering Manchester   117
59 Massabesic Lake   119
60 Portsmouth: A Visit to the Past   121
61 Exeter: String Bridge Walking Tour   125

Central New Hampshire
62 Point Trail and Lakeside Trail Loop   128
63 New Hampshire Winery   130
64 Welch-Dickey Loop Trail   132
65 Mt. Cardigan Summit   133
66 Concord: Coach and Eagle Trail   135

Southwestern New Hampshire
67 Mt. Monadnock   137

Northern New Hampshire
68 The Flume Path and the Pool   139
69 Lost River Gorge Walk   142
70 Lake Gloriette Trail   144
71 Mt. Washington: Alpine Garden Walk   146
72 A Walk to the Gorham Lead Mines   148

RHODE ISLAND

Eastern Rhode Island
73 A Stroll through Providence   150
74 Lincoln Woods   152

Southeastern Rhode Island
75 Colt Park and Prudence Island   153
76 Ruecker Wildlife Refuge   155

77	Fort Adams	156

Northern Rhode Island
78	Parker Woodland	158

Southern Rhode Island
79	Rodman's Hollow	160

Southwestern Rhode Island
80	Tippecansett Trail	162
81	Ben Utter Trail	164
82	John B. Hudson Trail	165
83	Breakheart Trail	166

Northeastern Rhode Island
84	Diamond Hill Trail	167

VERMONT

Central Vermont
85	Main Street, Poultney Village	169
86	Texas Falls	171
87	Robert Frost Trail	173
88	Lincoln Gap to Appalachian Gap: A Sampling of the Long Trail	175
89	Woodstock Walking Tour	178

Southern Vermont
90	Silver Lake Loop	180
91	Lye Brook Waterfalls	181
92	Townshend Forest Trail	183
93	Main Street, Windsor	185
94	Old Bennington	187

Northern Vermont
95	Stowe Recreation Path	189
96	Camel's Hump	191
97	Bayley Hazen Road to Greensboro	194
98	The Lake Loop	195
99	Nichols Ledge	198
100	Main Street, St. Johnsbury	200

Introduction

DRIVE/WALK AMERICA

Wanderlust, a phenomenon which has probably been part of the American psyche since the Pilgrims landed at Plymouth Rock, is at an all-time high in the United States. Americans, who were a little hesitant to jump into their cars for long drives during the oil crisis of the 1970s, are rediscovering the joys of driving. At the same time, perhaps with an eye on better fitness and good health, they have pushed walking into *first place* as their favorite exercise and recreational activity, according to the Bureau of the Census.

Combining walking and driving, while fairly new to the United States, has been common practice in Europe and countries such as New Zealand for many years. As you drive along certain highways in Europe, for example, you'll find rest stops where you can park your car and take a walk along a marked trail. At the Trailhead, a sign provides a map and indicates the distance of the walk, the approximate walking time, and the level of difficulty. In Austria and New Zealand, you can walk from city to city on specially created interconnecting walking routes.

Driving and walking are a good combination. Driving expands your walking horizons. You can "fast-forward" over areas you don't want to walk and spend more time enjoying those you do. Walking gives you an "intimate" view and a sense of place not attainable from a car that is whooshing along a highway. Getting out of your car, planting your feet solidly on the ground, taking a deep breath, and absorbing the sights and sounds around you can be an exhilarating experience and is, according to many, the best part of a travel day.

We hope to propel the walking movement in America toward a complete "foot network" across the United States with our *Walking Atlas of America* series. We started the process with *America's Greatest Walks* (Addison-Wesley, 1986) by placing signs at the beginning of some of the 100 walking routes described in that book.

Now we present 100 new walks in each region of the country: *Mid-America Walking Atlas*, *New England Walking Atlas*, and *California Walking Atlas*. Like the walk-route signs in Europe, these books provide a tableau of important information. Each description is accompanied by explicit driving directions from major roadways and cities, the approximate walking time, the mileage of the walk, the difficulty of the walk, and the best season to take it. One day we hope all the trails will be marked with our signs as part of a walking network, reaching across the country.

If you haven't yet made walking a daily habit on your business and vacation travels, here are our recommendations for fitting in a "walk a day":

- *Build time for a walk into your travel schedule by starting an hour earlier.* You'll be surprised how this extra margin will help you take advantage of an unplanned walking opportunity.

- *Be "walk-ready" at all times.* Wear walking shoes, socks, and comfortable clothing. Some people prefer to carry a backpack instead of a briefcase or pocketbook so they can take a walking break at a moment's notice. At any rate, travel "light."

- *Make a daily walk plan (even if it's only mental).* Think about each day, and decide when you might be able to take time out for a walk. Will it be in the morning before breakfast near your hotel? Can you walk to an appointment? Is there time at lunch? Before dinner? Maybe a "walking" meeting with a business associate? If you target the day's possible walking opportunities, you are more likely to actually find time to take your walk.

- *Be spontaneous.* Travelers—even though in the abstract they are seeking a pleasant escape or an exciting discovery—can get into a rut. The destination looms larger than the journey itself. Allow yourself the luxury of leaving your route, parking your car, and exploring a new area on foot.

NEW ENGLAND'S 100 BEST WALKS

New England—the term evokes picturesque towns with steepled churches and big white houses framing a lush Town Green; rolling green hills which turn brilliant orange, red, and yellow in the fall; quaint fishing villages; harbors, bays, and inlets; vast areas of unspoiled wilderness, covered bridges, river valleys, and mountain peaks. And history. New England is where America began, the repository of the country's early history, as well as the cultural and intellectual values that shaped it.

The walks in this book will take you on a journey through the six states of New England—Connecticut, Maine, Massachusetts, New Hampshire, Rhode Island, and Vermont—and will introduce you to the variety of the region's landscapes and the diversity of its people. The walks come from New Englanders or from people who love this part of the world, and whether you try one of these walks or take all of them, you will inevitably be caught up in the enthusiasm of those who shared their favorite walk with us.

Let's start with history. Brooks Kelly sent us a walk in Plymouth, Massachusetts, which begins, appropriately enough, where America's history began: Plymouth Rock. Polly Flansburgh nominated a walk through Boston's North End, which recaptures some of the feeling of revolutionary America. In addition to a visit to Copps Hill Burying Ground, where some of the tombstones are marked with bullet holes made by the British during target practice, the tour takes you by the Old North Church and through the winding seventeenth-century streets of Boston's oldest neighborhood. If you take Pat McCready's walk through Old Bennington, Vermont, you'll relive the famous Battle of Bennington during which 2,000 militiamen routed the British and turned the tide of war. Some of them may have received their training on the Town Green of Fairfield, Connecticut, where nominator Alex Billings tells us military drills were held in preparation for the revolution. Most of us have read about the Pilgrims and most of us know the facts behind the American Revolution, but Boston's Black Heritage Trail covers a part of history that most of us probably do not know very much about. Nominator Ken Heidelberg says, "The Black Heritage Trail deals with information not found in history books. Visitors get a personal touch they don't usually get."

To get a personal view of New England's influence on America's cultural development, you might take the Uptown Art Walk in Portland, Maine, which was nominated by Ralph Pride. John Marin,

Edward Hopper, Winslow Homer, and Andrew Wyeth are just a few of the artists who have established Maine as a vital center for art. New England's literary contribution can be sampled in a tour of the Mount—Edith Wharton's home in the Berkshire Hills of Massachusetts. Wharton, the first woman novelist to win a Pulitzer Prize, used the Berkshire countryside as a setting for many of her stories. Nominator Scott Marshall says: "It was—and still is—a place of creative energy, of great beauty, and of inspiration." Another inspiring walk with a literary bent is the Robert Frost Trail in the northern section of Vermont's Green Mountain National Forest. Frost's poetry is displayed on plaques along this walk, which received two nominations, one from Les Noble, who lives in nearby Middlebury and one from Penny Phillips, who discovered it while taking summer courses at Middlebury College Language School. "Everyone in my family says, 'Two roads diverged in a wood...' at every fork in every path," Penny told us, "so you can imagine that, for me, finding those words on a signpost in a wood seemed just like the way nature meant for a path to be. And, of course, the scenery is beautiful."

The beautiful New England scenery is perhaps most visited during the fall when nature puts on an unparalleled show of dazzling proportions. Any of the country or mountain walks described here would be wonderful in the fall. If you want to experience the colors up-close, take a walk in the woods, such as the Nichols Ledge Walk in Vermont's Northeast Kingdom, sent in by Natalie Kinsey-Warnock. For long-distance views of the foliage, try the Welch-Dickey Loop Trail nominated by Ned Therrien, which takes you into New Hampshire's White Mountains, or the walk nominated by David Reynolds, which follows the Perimeter Trail in the Rock Spring Wildlife Refuge along the Little River and up a steep hill to one of the most spectacular views in eastern Connecticut.

New England's villages are beautiful in the fall, but their unique charm is evident year-round, and is lovingly preserved by their twentieth-century residents. Stonington Borough, for example, is one of the most picturesque seaside towns in Connecticut, and its history as an eighteenth-century fishing village and as a nineteenth-century shipbuilding and whaling center can be seen firsthand on the walk submitted by Harriett Bessette. With characteristic "Yankee Pride," nominator Steve Flagg says his hometown of Wolfeboro, New Hampshire, on Lake Winnipesaukee, is not to be missed. "It's the most beautiful town to drive into," he says. "It rises up on a hill from the water and looks just like a postcard." And in Stowe, Vermont, the people liked their town so much they decided to build their own walking path. "Stowe's pride in this path," says nominator Anne Lusk, "has been evident not only by the town's willingness to fund and build it, but also by its eagerness to share it with visitors and by its desire to tell others how they, too, can build a path or 'greenway.'" Another Vermont village, Woodstock, nestled in the foothills of the Green Mountains, is thought by many to be the prettiest town in America. Nominator Sam Merlo certainly thinks so; his walk captures not only the beauty of today's Woodstock, but some of its past as well.

The village walks, and those in New England's cities, also give you a chance to sample seventeenth- and eighteenth-century architecture. Some of these old buildings are open to the public; many of them house period furniture or feature special exhibits. On Juliet Kellogg's tour of Bangor, Maine, for example, you'll find a diversity of architecture which reflects the city's history, including the elegant mansions of Bangor's lumber barons. Jim Garvin sent us a walk in Portsmouth, New Hampshire, which takes you by one of the grandest Georgian mansions in New England, and on John Flaherty's stroll through Providence, Rhode Island, you can go inside an eighteenth-century home that John Quincy Adams thought was one of the most elegant he had ever seen. Patricia Endlich sent us a walk in Poultney Village, Vermont, which highlights the town's architectural diversity from Victorian homes to Greek Revival, Italianate, and Queen Anne styles. In Old Bennington, Vermont, you'll find the largest concentration of early Georgian and Federal homes in the state, and on the tour of Boston's North End, you'll see Paul Revere's house, which was built around 1680; Revere bought it in 1770. The style of the house is medieval, often called "memory style," because it reflects the memories the colonists had of their homes in England.

Many of the nominations we received were for walks along the coast. David Costa sent us a walk on Crescent Beach in northeast Maine, which he says is "one of the most beautiful places on earth." Nominator Beverly Meltzer-Boxtein might not disagree, but she omits the qualifier when describing her favorite walk: "Old Orchard Beach is the most beautiful beach in the world!" Maine's harbortown of Kennebunkport received two nominations: Mary Folsom especially likes it in winter when it's quiet, but Bob Ellis likes it all year. "There is no place more beautiful than Kennebunkport!" he exclaims. Rhode Island, the "Ocean State," is a good place for water walks, and we received several. Kevin O'Malley sent us a walk on Prudence Island, which can be reached only by ferry, and Al Hawkes told us about

Ruecker Wildlife Refuge, where you can observe heron and a variety of shorebirds in a salt marsh and walk along the beach looking for fiddler crabs.

Walking is a wonderful way to see things you may have missed before. When John Brodhead injured himself running, he decided to take his "running" route—the Lake Loop in Craftsbury Common, Vermont—at a slower pace. "The contrasts between running the Lake Loop and walking it immediately began to impress me," he recalls. "Traveling at one-third my accustomed rate over this familiar route opened my eyes to an entirely different scene." Other walkers have discovered a "magic" in the companionship walking affords. When Lorraine Hanson takes her daily walk on Mackworth Island, Maine, she meets a lot of people. "No celebrities," she says, "but just a lot of nice people." Elissa Silvio likes to take the 6-mile hike up Massachusetts' Mt. Greylock as much for the people she meets as for the views. "At just about any time of year, you'll meet up with Appalachian Trail 'through hikers,'" she explains. "Their stories are as interesting as the views are spectacular." Flora Pignatiello sent us a wonderful walk along the Charles River in Boston. She and her walking group, known as Champions on Foot, meet every Tuesday, rain or shine, to walk. "We have become a family," she says, "sharing many of the same interests. Our weekly walks have brought back the sense of humor some of us had lost due to the loneliness that is very often the major pain of being an elder. The walks have somehow brought out our 'hidden talents.'"

We hope you enjoy these walks in New England as much as the people who told us about them do. Look for them along the trails!

If you have a favorite walk that you would like to share, please complete the form at the end of the book and send it to us. We'd also appreciate any suggestions or updated information you might have on the walks in this book.

The maps are meant to give you a general orientation to each new area. We suggest you obtain more detailed information locally when you arrive, to ensure that you make the most of your visit. There are many self-guided tour brochures and trail guides which will enhance your walks.

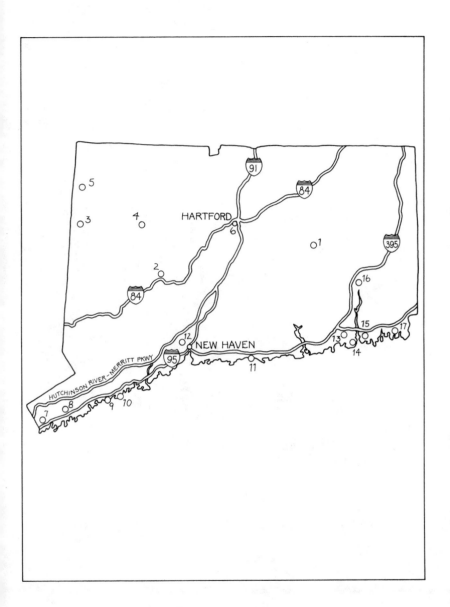

Connecticut

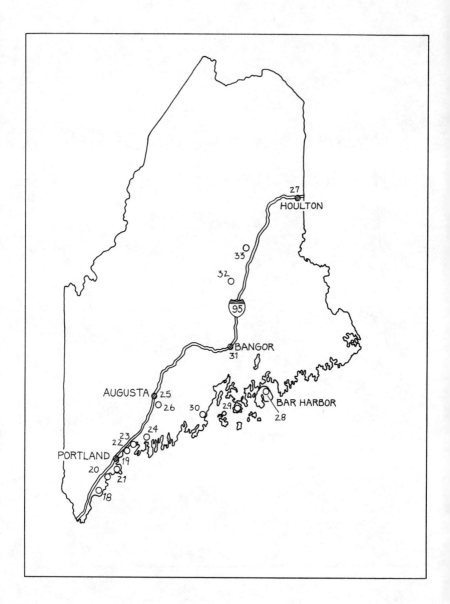

Maine

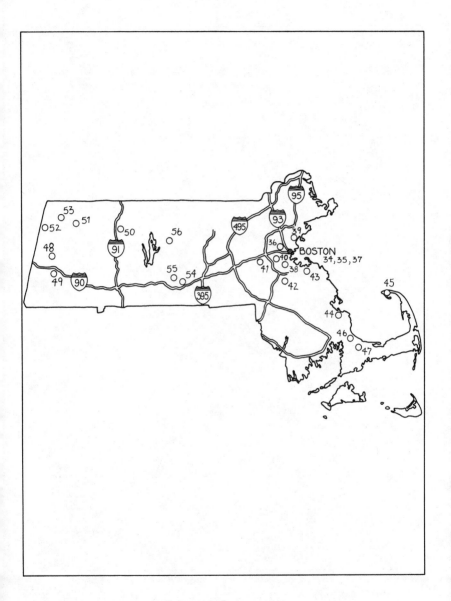

Massachusetts

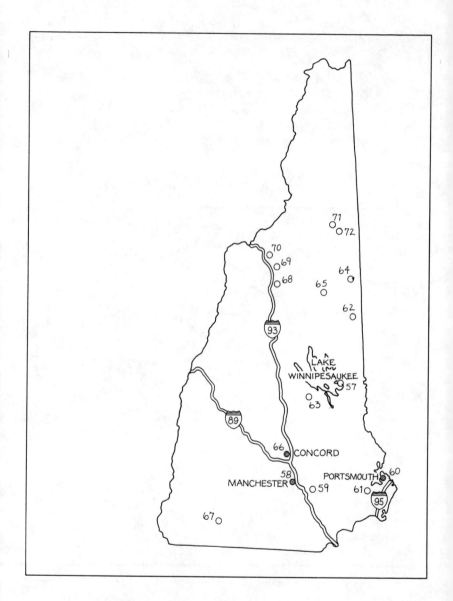

New Hampshire

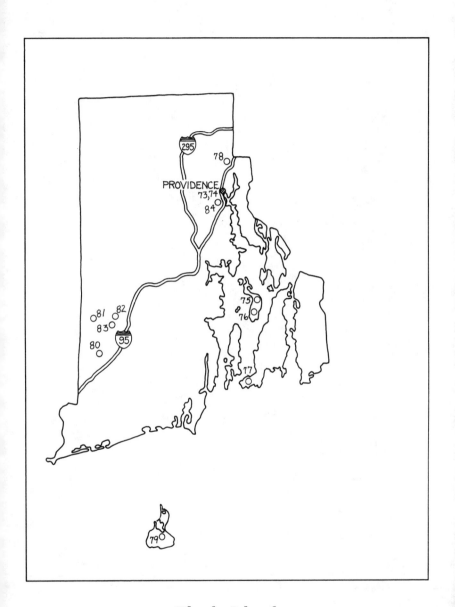

Rhode Island

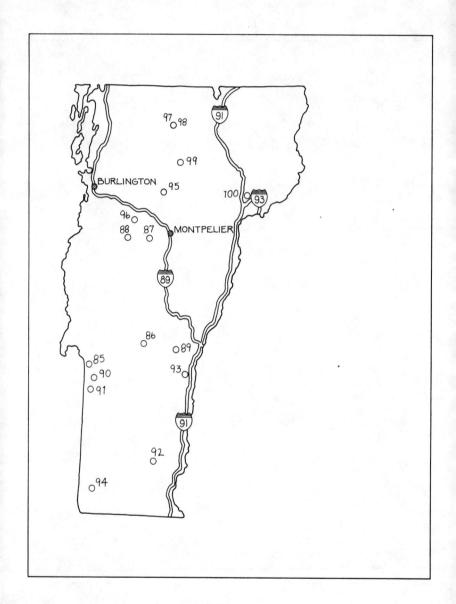

Vermont

Connecticut

EASTERN CONNECTICUT

Rock Spring Wildlife Refuge: Perimeter Trail (1)

Directions: The Rock Spring Wildlife Refuge is located near the town of Scotland, off Route 97. From Willimantic, take Route 6 east, and turn right on Route 14. Drive east on 14 through Windham and Scotland, and turn left (north) on Route 97 (Puddinghill Road) toward Hampton. The refuge will be on your right, about 1.5 miles from Route 14.

Best Season: Year-round; the views in the fall are the most spectacular.

Length: 3 miles round-trip. Allow an hour or two.

Degree of Difficulty: Easy to moderate; along the river there can be heavy brush on the trail.

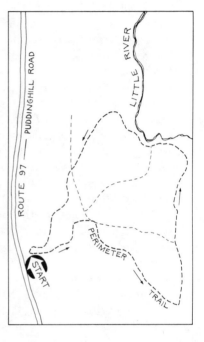

Highlights: "This is an area where people can be in communion with nature," says nominator David Reynolds. "There is a wide variety of terrain and the refuge is a sanctuary for several endangered plants and animals."

The 3-mile loop Perimeter Trail is marked with white blazes. From the parking area, stop by the display board that shows the trail system and pick up a trail map. You should also sign in here so that the refuge can keep track of the number of people who visit. Note that there are two shortcuts back to the parking area if you prefer not to make the full 3-mile loop.

1

The first part of the trail passes through a mixed oak and hickory forest. Follow the white blazes along the wide trail past a vernal pond, out of the forest, and into an open field. Watch for deer, rabbits, and other wildlife. Before long, you'll come to Indian Spring. Walk downstream a little way to see the spring bubbling up from the sand.

From Indian Spring, follow the trail up the slope of the *esker,* a geologic feature that was formed when the glaciers melted and left hollow channels which were later filled with sand and gravel. The soil on top of the esker contains very little organic material and is excessively drained. As a result, trees tend to be dwarfed, and the vegetation is scanty.

At the foot of the esker is a pine plantation where rows and rows of pine trees stand about three feet apart. Pine needles have formed a dense bed on the forest floor, and the atmosphere is hushed. "It's like entering a cavernous European cathedral," remarks nominator David Reynolds, who suggests you sit quietly on the soft pine needles for a while and watch for wildlife. You may see an owl or two or a raccoon. Once David saw three roughed grouse, which are not common in Connecticut.

At the northern end of the pine plantation, follow the trail left across a bridge of fallen logs and head upstream along the Little River (look for the beaver dam). The trail follows the river for about ½ mile and climbs a steep hill to the top, where you'll enjoy one of the most spectacular views in eastern Connecticut. From this peaceful vantage point overlooking the Little River Valley, you can experience a "communion with nature." Hawks may soar overhead, and if there is no wind, you will be able to hear the gurgling sounds of the Little River as it makes its way through the valley below.

From the hilltop, follow the trail downhill through the woods to the parking area.

WESTERN CONNECTICUT

Downtown Waterbury (2)

Directions: Waterbury is located at the junction of I-84 and Route 8. The walk begins at the Mattatuck Museum, 144 West Main Street.

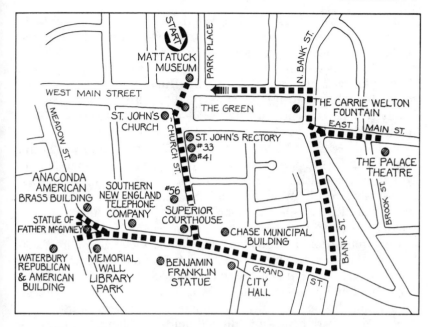

Best Season: Year-round, but spring is especially lovely, and at Christmastime, the Green is ablaze with life.

Length: About 3 miles. Allow approximately one hour.

Degree of Difficulty: Easy.

Highlights: Architectural diversity blends the old and the new on this tour of the city once known as the "Brass Capital of the World."

The Mattatuck Museum, where this walk begins, is the only museum in Connecticut dedicated exclusively to the state's art and history. In addition to exhibits, you'll also find the Waterbury Convention & Visitors Commission here. This walk, nominated by Barbara Sticco, highlights some of the stops along a much more detailed self-guided walk; for the complete brochure, stop in at the Convention & Visitors Commission.

Opposite the museum, note the Soldiers Monument, one of the few Civil War memorials to depict a theme of a united nation. The sculptor, George E. Bissell, was a Waterbury native. Cross West Main Street to the southwestern tip of the Green where a granite memorial in the grass reads: "The present settlement of Waterbury was made on land in this region. The original settlement [in 1674], known as Town Plot, was abandoned during the King Philip's War, and the town site changed to this location in 1677." The Green itself is a lovely two-acre downtown park, originally used by farmers as grazing land.

Walk across West Main Street to Church Street. Here you'll find many beautiful old homes and a view of St. John's Episcopal Church, which boasts a classic clock steeple and several Tiffany windows. Across the street from the church is St. John's Rectory, a fine example of the "Richardsonian" Romanesque style of architecture. The rectory has recently been restored for use as an office building.

Church Street still retains the charm of the Victorian era in Waterbury, and the next two homes at 33 and 41 Church Street, which were built just after the Civil War, are good examples of that style. The building at 56 Church Street, near Grand, is a house reminiscent of an Italian villa. It now houses the offices of Catholic Family Services.

Providing stark contrast to the old homes of Church Street is the contemporary Superior Courthouse at 300 Grand Street. To the west of the courthouse, adding a touch of elegance, is the Southern New England Telephone Company Building, a Georgian structure built in 1931. The semicircular brick building that rounds from Grand Street onto Meadow Street was the headquarters of the Anaconda American Brass Company from 1913 until it was sold a few years ago. This unusual building is an impressive reminder of Waterbury's past as the "Brass Capital of the World." Another impressive and unusual building can be seen across Meadow Street. This Italian Renaissance Revival structure, with its 240-foot-high clock tower, was completed in 1909 at a cost of $332,000. It was once the city's train station and now houses Waterbury's daily newspapers.

Cross Meadow Street to the brick wall of Library Park, noting the bronze statue of Reverend Michael J. McGivney, a Waterbury native and founder of the Knights of Columbus, and the statue of Benjamin Franklin sitting on a bench in the library's plaza. Head east from the park on Grand Street to see the buildings of the Cass Gilbert Historic District, all listed in the *National Register of Historic Places*. Architect Cass Gilbert designed both the magnificent City Hall at 235

Grand Street as well as the Chase Municipal Building across the street and several other buildings along Grand and Field streets. Many think the City Hall is the most attractive municipal government center in New England. Note the Italian sunken garden in the central enclosure.

Turn left on Bank Street and walk to East Main. Turn right and walk past Brook Street to the Palace Theatre at 100 East Main. This is the "star" of East Main Street's restoration. One of the largest theaters in New England, it was constructed in 1922. Restoration of the rectory and Frederick buildings was also recently completed. It is estimated that the complete restoration project will cost $16.5 million.

Retrace your steps back East Main to North Bank Street and turn right. Cross North Bank for an up-close look at a Waterbury landmark which has come to symbolize the city—the Carrie Welton Fountain. It was donated in 1888 by Carrie Welton and dedicated to the people of Waterbury in the name of her favorite stallion, Knight. A walk down West Main Street will take you back to the Mattatuck Museum, where the walk began.

Before you leave Waterbury, be sure to visit the splendid Immaculate Conception Church on the Green. Executed in the grand basilica style of Saint Mary Major in Rome, "The Immaculate" welcomes visitors of all faiths.

WESTERN CONNECTICUT

Kent to Cornwall Bridge: A Walk on the Appalachian Trail (3)

Directions: Kent is located on Route 7 at the western edge of Connecticut, near the New York border. From the traffic light, drive west on Route 341, cross the bridge, and turn right along the river road. Take the dirt road which forks to your right after ½ mile, and drive another 2½ miles to the parking area, where the Appalachian Trail comes off the ledges on your left and then follows the road.

Best Season: Year-round, weather permitting; each season has its own unique beauty.

Length: About 4.8 miles to Swift's Bridge, where you can arrange to have another car parked. Cornwall Bridge is about another 3 miles along the road for a total distance of 7.8 miles one way. From there you can return to Swift's Bridge and drive back to Kent (if you've arranged for a car to be there), or you can spend the night in Cornwall Bridge and retrace your steps back to Kent the next day. If you start early in the morning, you can make the round-trip walk in one day.

Degree of Difficulty: Easy.

Highlights: Scenic views and a wonderful country feeling make this walk—the longest river walk on the Appalachian Trail—special.

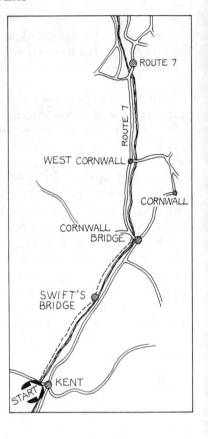

On this walk, the Appalachian Trail follows the west bank of the Housatonic River from the picturesque town of Kent to Cornwall Bridge. You'll pass through hardwood forests and stands of hemlock, and you'll have lovely views of the river.

When you come to the remnants of North Kent Bridge, which once spanned the Housatonic, the Appalachian Trail passes through a gate. Continue straight ahead on the road, which eventually becomes a dirt path and goes through meadows and woods to another paved road. The river is your companion the entire distance; most of the way it's peaceful, adding a melancholy feeling to this lovely walk, but it gets a little restless as it approaches Cornwall Bridge. You'll see the rapids near Swift's Bridge frequently dotted with canoeists and kayakers enjoying an exhilarating ride in the fast-moving waters. Follow the road under a river bridge to Route 7 and turn left, crossing the bridge into Cornwall Bridge Village.

The Appalachian Trail, which stretches some 2,000 miles from Maine to Georgia, is the only National Scenic Trail in the northeast. It originated in the mind of Benton MacKaye (rhymes with "sky"), who loved the outdoors and envisioned a footpath from New Hampshire to North Carolina, where people could escape from "the scramble of everyday worldly commercial life." The implementation of MacKaye's vision began in 1923, and his original concept grew to encompass fourteen states. In 1925, the Appalachian Conference was formed to help protect and maintain the trail. Today the Appalachian Trail, the granddaddy of long-distance trails in America, is a tribute to MacKaye, and it is a wonderful experience for thousands of hiking enthusiasts.

When you return to Kent, drive north on Route 7 to Kent Falls State Park where you'll find the largest waterfall in Connecticut. There is a steep path leading to the top of the 200-foot-high falls. From here, surrounded by lush green foliage with sun peeping through the leaves, you'll have a perfect view of the water cascading down over a series of rock ledges.

WESTERN CONNECTICUT

The White Memorial Foundation (4)

Directions: The foundation is located 2 miles west of the town of Litchfield on Route 202. From Hartford, take Route 4 west to Route 118. Follow 118 to Route 202 in Litchfield and turn west. From Waterbury, take Route 8 north to exit 42 (Route 118).

Best Season: Year-round.

Length: Varies; there are more than 35 miles of trails through a variety of terrain. Plan on spending at least half a day here.

Degree of Difficulty: Easy to difficult.

Highlights: A chance to explore meadows, ponds, and streams in a pristine 4,000-acre lakeshore sanctuary.

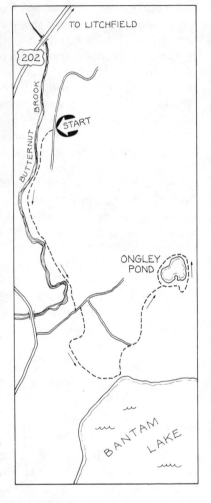

With foresight and a commitment to conservation, two former Litchfield residents, Alain White and his sister May White, decided that beautiful Bantam Lake should be preserved so that people would be able to enjoy and appreciate its unspoiled lake and woodland character for generations to come. Between 1908 and 1912 the Whites purchased land around the lake, and in 1913 they established The White Memorial Foundation, which today comprises some 4,000 acres of fields, waters, and woodland. In addition, the Whites gave an endowment to assist in the maintenance and development of the foundation, which is guided by four major principles: recreation, education, conservation, and research. "This was such a wonderful gift to the town," says nominator Janet Serra, "and it's never crowded because it's so big."

A museum features interpretive exhibits as well as live owls, reptiles, and other animals, authentically depicted dioramas of Bantam Lake scenes, and an excellent nature library. Nearby the Holbrook Bird Observatory overlooks an area that has been specially landscaped to attract a variety of birds at different seasons throughout the year. With thirty sheltered viewing stations, this is an outstanding place for bird-watchers to observe and take photographs.

There are more than twenty marked trails in the preserve, ranging in length from under ½ mile to just over 6 miles. There is also a special nature trail for the blind and a boardwalk trail that overlooks a marsh pond. One of Janet's favorite walks links the ½-mile Butternut Brook Trail with the Lake Trail, then loops back on the Windmill Hill Trail, and circles Ongley Pond. The total distance is under 2 miles, and the walk offers wonderful changes in terrain; there is a shaded pathway along Butternut Brook, an observation platform over Bantam Lake, and an up-close look at pond life.

Picnicking, boating, and camping are all available here. Advance registration is required for camping. Call (203) 567-0089 for information or write: The White Memorial Foundation and Conservation Center, P.O. Box 368, Litchfield, CT 06759.

After your visit to The White Memorial Foundation, be sure to stop in the beautiful old town of Litchfield and walk around the Village Green and along North and South streets. The Tapping Reeve House on South Street (open to the public from mid-May to mid-October) is filled with late eighteenth-century furnishings. Adjacent to the house is the one-room office of Judge Tapping Reeve, who started the country's first law school in 1774. There are ten churches in Litchfield; note the beautiful double-octagon steeple of the First Congregational Church on the Green.

NORTHWESTERN CONNECTICUT

Bog Meadow Trail (5)

Directions: The walk is located in the Northeast Audubon Center in Sharon. From I-84, take Route 4 west. Trails are open daily, dawn to dusk.

Best Season: Year-round, but the foliage is magnificent in the fall.

Length: The walk to Bog Meadow is about 1¼ miles. Allow an hour to an hour and a half.

Degree of Difficulty: Moderate.

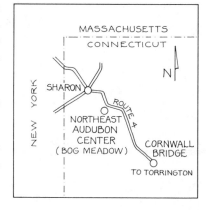

Highlights: Diversity of habitats and various plants and animals native to the northeast are the highlights of this walk.

Encompassing nearly 700 acres of scenic Connecticut countryside, the Northeast Audubon Center is a wonderful place to bring the whole family for a walk. Half the property has been designated as a natural area, and is a sanctuary in the true sense of the word; the other half contains some 11 miles of footpaths where you can appreciate nature up-close and firsthand. There are a number of different habitats, including pond and stream, field and forest, and marshland; each one supports its own varieties of plant and animal life. Plant life varies from striped maples to sphagnum moss, and animals you might see include beavers, deer, and wild turkeys. Birds vary with the seasons and include osprey, Canada geese, and a wide variety of songbirds. At one time much of this land was settled; today the old stone walls that cross the property and the charcoal mounds you see here and there are reminders of this history.

Nominator Valerie Grustas particularly likes the Bog Meadow Trail. The route is clearly marked from the parking area, where a map displays the various pathways. The Bog Meadow Trail continues along the boardwalk, by a pond, where you'll find ducks, turtles, mink, and beavers. Photographers will be delighted by the natural beauty. "It's especially nice after a rainstorm," Valerie says, "because more of the animals can be seen then. Squirrels, chipmunks, and deer will scurry right across the path in front of you."

When you get back to the Audubon Center, be sure to stop in to see the exhibits there, or visit the gift shop. You may even be fortunate enough to see two nonexhibit animals: Rasta, an arctic wolf, and Wolfie, a red wolf. Valerie, the Audubon staff, and the wolves hit the trail daily for a "wolf walk."

CENTRAL CONNECTICUT

The Walk, Hartford (6)

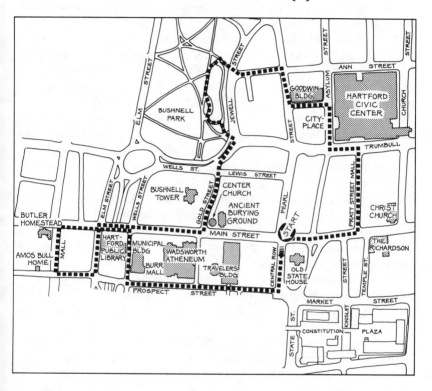

Directions: The major highways emptying into downtown Hartford are I-91 (north/south) and I-84 (east/west). The Walk begins at the Old State House on State Street.

Best Season: The Walk can be enjoyed at any time of year, but it's best when the sun is shining. It gets cold in Hartford in the winter, but a crisp, clear winter day makes for great walking.

Length: 3 to 4 miles. Allow at least two to three hours and much more if you plan to take some of the side tours along the way.

Degree of Difficulty: Easy.

Highlights: This walk offers a sampling of architectural diversity in Connecticut's capital.

This historic city walk was nominated by Elizabeth Shluger of Marlborough, Connecticut, who was particularly fascinated by the architecture of the old buildings in Connecticut's capital city. The Old State House, for example, where The Walk begins, was the first public building designed by Charles Bulfinch, who was to exert enormous influence on Colonial architecture and was the designer, among other things, of the Capitol Building in Washington, D.C.

It is significant that Hartford's Walk should begin at the Old State House in what is now called Thomas Hooker Square, for in 1636, Thomas Hooker, a Puritan clergyman, left his home in Cambridge, Massachusetts, with a group of discontented families, and walked to a place that was then known as *Suckiag* (an Indian word meaning "black earth"). Hooker later renamed Suckiag "Hartford" after Hertford, England. The Walk commemorates the historic journey of Hooker, a founder of Connecticut, and his friends. At another point along the route, Center Church, you can see the site where Hooker is thought to have been buried.

The Walk is a self-guided tour. Pick up your tour guide brochure at the Old State House between 10 a.m. and 5 p.m. Monday through Saturday or between 12 and 5 p.m. on Sunday. The brochure is full of information and historic details.

One of the highlights along The Walk is the Wadsworth Atheneum, which definitely merits a side tour of its own. Inside you'll find forty-seven galleries with 165 permanent and visiting exhibits, including period costumes, furniture, sculpture, and a hands-on exhibit you are encouraged to touch. The museum is closed on Mondays; the hours Tuesday through Sunday are from 11 a.m. to 5 p.m. There is a $3 admission fee for adults; children under 13 get in free.

Art lovers will also be delighted to discover a work by Alexander Calder: the *Stegosaurus* can be seen at Burr Mall, a small space in between the Wadsworth Atheneum and the Municipal Building.

The Travelers Insurance Companies Tower building is on the site of the old Sanford's Tavern. Here, in 1687, Captain Joseph Wadsworth took Connecticut's Charter and hid it in an oak tree to keep it out of the hands of England's James II. The Royal Governor took over the state for two years, but he was never able to take over the Charter. You can see this Royal Oak Charter in the Hartford Public Library, another point of interest along The Walk.

Another not-to-be-missed part of The Walk is Bushnell Park, 37 acres of green space within the city. Children and adults alike will enjoy the Bushnell Park Carousel one of the few old-time merry-go-rounds left in existence. Of interest, too, in Bushnell Park is the Corning Fountain, a 30-foot fountain of tall Indian maidens and crouching braves, which pays tribute to the American Indian.

When you have finished The Walk, be sure to stop by Elizabeth Park at Prospect and Asylum streets, in the west end of the city. Here you'll find about 14,000 rose plants with 1,000 different varieties. There are four greenhouses with hundreds of other colorful plants in addition to the spectacular roses.

SOUTHWESTERN CONNECTICUT

Greenwich Point (7)

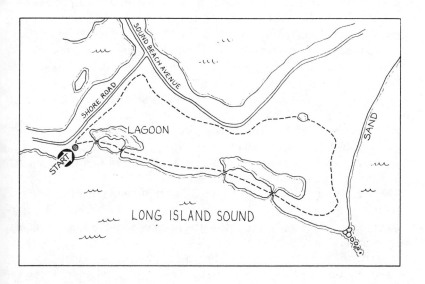

Directions: Greenwich Point is located in the Old Greenwich section of Greenwich, the southernmost town in Fairfield County, about 28 miles east of New York City. Take I-95 to exit 5, and turn right onto Route 1 (East Putnam Avenue). Turn right at the first traffic light onto Sound Beach Avenue. Drive to the end of the road, which intersects with Shore Road; bear right, and follow the road for about ½ mile to the entrance (Tod's Driftway). This walk begins near the lagoon in the middle of Greenwich Point.

Best Season: Late winter and early spring. (Greenwich Point is open to residents of Greenwich only from April 1 to December 1.)

Length: About 5 miles. You could spend at least half a day at Greenwich Point; there are picnic tables and lots of places to observe the birds. The trail takes about one and a half to two hours.

Degree of Difficulty: Easy.

Highlights: This is a scenic walk along a beach on Long Island Sound.

Encompassing 147 acres, Greenwich Point is the largest shorefront park in the Town of Greenwich. It belonged to a wealthy banker named J. Kennedy Tod who left the property to the Presbyterian Hospital. In 1944, the hospital sold the point to the town with the promise that it would be preserved. Today residents enjoy the quiet beauty of Greenwich Point for walking, picnicking, jogging, bird watching, photography, nature study, swimming, and boating.

Nominator Douglas Krajewski says that the loop trail follows the shore of Long Island Sound, then turns inland briefly, before heading back along the opposite shore. Numbered markers correspond to descriptions found in a booklet entitled *A Guide to Greenwich Point*, which can be purchased for $1 at the Bookstore of Old Greenwich, 237 Sound Beach Avenue, Old Greenwich.

The first part of the trail is along dikes that were constructed several years ago from rocks, stones, gravel, and soil to protect the point from erosion. When you get to the first bridge, note the salt marsh on the right. This was established in 1975, and became the first proof in the state of Connecticut that a salt marsh could be successfully created in an area disturbed by humans. Salt water cordgrass is slowly spreading, hampered only by Canada geese, which feed on the roots of young plants.

From the second bridge, look down on the rocks in the sound, where you can see rockweed. The plant is easily recognized by the series of what are called *air bladders* along the stem. These bladders make the plant float upward when the tide comes in so that all sides of the plant come in contact with water. On the other side of this bridge you may see some sea lettuce. These are actually pieces that have broken off a sea lettuce plant, which grows entirely underwater. These pieces decay and become food for fish and animals. There is an enormous diversity of life at Greenwich Point, from an estimated 200 varieties of birds to numerous kinds of shellfish.

As you head inland along the trail, you'll come to a large boulder on top of a hill. This became a memorial to Mr. Tod after his death in 1925, and also commemorates the purchase of the territory known today as Old Greenwich from the Indians in 1640. The land, including the point, was bought by Captain Daniel Patrick and Robert and Elizabeth Feake for twenty-five English coats, a sobering thought when you consider the value of real estate in Greenwich today!

Farther along the trail you'll come to a grove of holly trees, which includes twenty-one different varieties. The grove, a gift from Mr. and Mrs. Allan Kitchel on the occasion of their fiftieth wedding anniversary, becomes a winter hiding place for the saw-whet owl, the smallest of the owls who live in this area.

At the end of the trail, spend some time at the lagoon to watch the egrets and black-crowned night herons, who are enjoying the place as much as you.

SOUTHWESTERN CONNECTICUT

Mianus River Gorge: Brink of Gorge Trail (8)

Directions: The gorge is located in Stamford. Take the Merritt Parkway to exit 34, Long Ridge Road, and drive north to Miller Falls Road. Turn left onto Miller Falls, then left again on Mianus River Road. The parking area for the gorge is on the left.

Best Season: Spring and fall.

Length: 5 miles round-trip; allow half a day.

Degree of Difficulty: Easy.

Highlights: Along this walk you'll pass through a variety of natural habitats from forest and woodland to rocky areas and riverbeds.

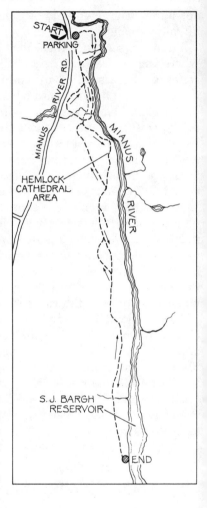

"This walk is an almost solitary experience with nature," says nominator Jeff O'Donnell. "You rarely see other people, and there are no commercial activities."

At the parking area, you can view an informative diorama depicting the history of the area and you can pick up a trail map there as well. The Brink of Gorge Trail leaves from the shelter and enters a pine knoll. The Nature Conservancy has labeled many of the plants, trees, and shrubs all along the trail, so anyone who is interested can learn what the different plants are. More than 100 varieties of trees, shrubs, and vines have been found and identified as well as some 250 wildflowers and over 100 species of birds.

From the pine knoll, you'll enter a forest filled with hemlock (the largest tree in the gorge is a hemlock estimated to be 300 years old). Follow the lower trail along the Mianus River for about ¾ mile. (The river takes its name from Myanos, who was chief of the Mohican Indian tribe, which lived in the area.) Note the ferns and skunk cabbage along the riverbank. Then the trail climbs to an overlook which affords views of the river as it breaks out of the gorge. Jeff says he especially likes to be here at sunrise or sunset. To return, follow the high trail along the top of the gorge and back to the parking area.

Mianus Gorge was formed 10,000 to 15,000 years ago when glaciers covering the area began to melt and the rushing water poured through the rock. Over time, the water eroded the rock more and more, leaving the long, narrow channel you see today. In fact, the process of erosion is not over.

The gorge is maintained by the Nature Conservancy as a "wilderness island." This means that the area is to be left alone, to "live so far as possible free from any interference by man directly or indirectly while the tract develops along wholly natural lines, regardless of what these may prove to be." Today there are many such areas throughout the United States, but the Mianus River Gorge was the Nature Conservancy's pioneer land project and became the country's first registered Natural History Landmark in 1964.

SOUTHWESTERN CONNECTICUT

Sherwood Island Shore Walk (9)

Directions: This walk is located in Sherwood Island State Park, 2 miles south of Westport. Take exit 18 off I-95 (Connecticut Turnpike), and watch for signs to Sherwood Island, which is connected by a causeway to the mainland.

Best Season: Spring or fall (the summer can be hot and crowded).

Length: About 1½ miles. Allow about an hour for a leisurely stroll.

Degree of Difficulty: Easy.

Highlights: This walk along the shore of Long Island Sound can be

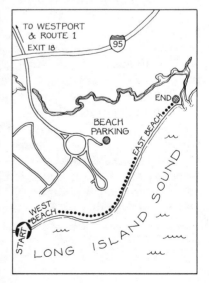

a relaxing stroll, a fun-filled family walk, or a fast-paced walking workout; it's up to you.

Nominator Glenn Miller likes to start this walk at the end of West Beach, where the sand is white and the beach is fairly isolated. There are some rocky areas here, but not too many. Glenn suggests you take a swim in the beautiful, clear water before beginning your walk along the shore to the East Beach.

A tidal salt marsh surrounds much of the 234-acre Sherwood Island. It provides a feeding and nesting habitat for migratory ducks, herons, and egrets, and offers a wonderful opportunity for walkers to watch and photograph these waterfowl. Canada geese and mute swans are year-round residents.

Near the West Beach is a wooded area of oak and hickory that may have reminded the Sherwoods, among the first families to settle in Fairfield around 1643, of their home in Old England, Sherwood Forest (of Robin Hood fame). Daniel Sherwood was the first homesteader on Sherwood Island, but long before he got there, the Indians had used the island for bathing, fishing, and bird hunting.

Today the island is for fun, and millions enjoy its beaches, groves, and meadows annually. There are several picnic areas and refreshment stands around the island, and shore fishing is very popular, especially in the fall when bluefish, striped bass, flounder, and blackfish can be found just offshore. But of all the activities enjoyed on Sherwood Island, nothing quite compares to a brisk, early-morning walk on the beach. If you time it just right, you can be the first one there. Start at West Beach and walk the 1.5 miles to the end of East Beach where you can refresh with a swim before walking back; it's a great way to start the day!

After your walk, you may enjoy visiting the town of Westport, where you can browse through a variety of interesting shops, including the Remarkable Bookshop, housed in an intriguing pink gingerbreadlike house. Also, if you're in Westport during the summer, don't miss the wonderful Westport Playhouse, which features some of the best in summer theater. For more information call (203) 226-6983.

SOUTHWESTERN CONNECTICUT

A Walking Tour of Fairfield (10)

Directions: Fairfield is about an hour and a half drive from New York City. Take exit 22 (Round Hill Road) off I-95 and turn right. Go straight, under the railroad trestle, and cross Post Road. At the next intersection (Beach Road and Old Post Road), you'll see the Town Green and Town Hall ahead of you. The Fairfield Historical Society is to your right (next to the church on the corner); park here.

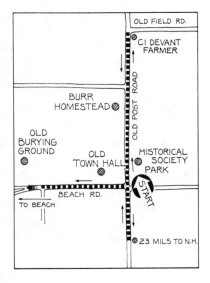

Best Season: Spring through fall.

Length: The walk to the beach is about 2 miles, but allow at least half a day for this tour of Fairfield, more if you plan to take a picnic and hike along the beach.

Degree of Difficulty: Easy.

Highlights: Fairfield is a beautiful, quintessential New England town. This walk combines history with colonial folklore and a nice stroll along Long Island Sound.

From the Historical Society parking lot, walk right onto the Old Post Road, which was once a Pequot Indian Trail, and pause for a moment to consider a bit of history. In August 1639, the Pequot Indians sold *Uncowaye* (an Indian word meaning "looking forward—a valley") to Roger Ludlowe, who had visited the area during the Pequot Indian Campaign in 1637 and was attracted by the area's beautiful natural harbors. Shortly thereafter, Uncowaye became known as Fairfield.

Walk to the corner of Old Post Road and Old Field Road where you'll come across a marker which has remained a mystery for almost 200 years. The marker reads: "David Barlow, the ci devant (meaning "former") farmer, 1791." No one knows why this stone marker was erected. Some think it may have denoted a property line (an early "No Trespassing" sign); others believe it may have been put up by Americans who were sympathetic to the French Revolution.

Cross to the other side of the Old Post Road, and retrace your steps back to the Burr Homestead. The mansion you see was built by Thaddeus Burr in 1790; the Doric columns were added in 1840. The original Burr Homestead, built in 1732, had served as a place of refuge for John Hancock, Samuel Adams, Dorothy Quincy (Hancock's fiancée), and Hancock's Aunt Lydia during the British occupation of Boston in May of 1775. Eventually the British burned it down, but not before John and Dorothy held their wedding reception there.

Continue down the Old Post Road to the Town Green, where military drills were held in preparation for the French and Indian War and the Revolutionary War. Note the Whipping Post which faces the First Congregational Church. Punishments were carried out at the post for such crimes as swearing and drunkenness, and the post was used to display town notices. Punishment is no longer meted out here, but town notices are still posted.

Cross Beach Road, and look for a stone marker near the Sherman Parsonage at 480 Old Post Road. The marker reads: "23 Mils to N.H.," and according to legend, Benjamin Franklin, who was Postmaster General in 1753, traveled the main roads with an invention of his own that recorded the number of miles, so that markers like this one could be placed to fix postage rates by weight and distance. In fact, the markers were required by Connecticut statute.

The Town Hall in the middle of the Green was built in 1794 to replace the original house which had been destroyed by fire by the British during their attack on Fairfield in 1779. The building was enlarged in 1870 in the French Second Empire style and restored to its original eighteenth-century elegance in 1930. Walk through the Town Hall parking lot to see Fairfield's colonial "claim to fame," the Sun Tavern, where George Washington stopped to eat in 1789.

Walk down Beach Road to the Old Burying Ground. This is the part of the walk nominator Alex Billings likes best. "Two large trees shade a large part of the yard," she says, "making this a perfect place for a picnic." The oldest tombstone reads: "S.M., 1687." Many of the stones are decorated with the Angel of Death or with the Skull and Crossbones, popular in the 1700s, but there are also examples of the Weeping Willow stones of the 1800s. Anthropologists point to such gravestones as an indication of society's changing attitudes about death. For those who find a visit to a graveyard somewhat morbid, Alex suggests you heed the words on the tombstone of Abel Wheeler: "Hark from the tombs a doleful sound, my ears attend the cry. Ye living men come view the ground where you must shortly lie."

From the graveyard, continue down Beach Road to Jennings Beach and Long Island Sound. A wooden boardwalk leads over small dunes, recently "built" and planted with seagrass to fight beach erosion. The walk to the beach is about 2 miles, but you can extend it with a beach walk of several more miles, if you wish.

SOUTH CENTRAL CONNECTICUT

Willard's Island (11)

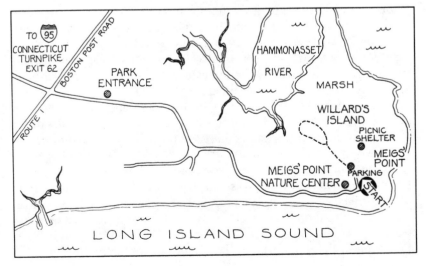

Directions: The walk is located in Hammonasset Beach State Park in Madison. From I-95, take exit 62, and drive south. At the junction with Route 1, go straight across the intersection and enter the park. Leave your car in the upper portion of Meigs' Point parking lot, and look for the orange gate to Willard's Island.

Best Season: You can take this walk year-round, but the best seasons for bird-watchers are spring and fall when warbler migrations are heaviest. The Meigs' Point Nature Center is open Tuesdays through Sundays, 10 a.m. to 5 p.m. from mid-May to mid-September.

Length: ½ mile; allow about half an hour.

Degree of Difficulty: Easy.

Highlights: Willard's Island is a bird lover's paradise, and the salt marsh affords an opportunity to experience an interesting and relatively unique habitat.

Willard's Island is part of Hammonasset Beach State Park. At one time it was a campground, and so there is a paved road that crosses the salt marsh to the island, which is open only to pedestrians and nature. Some of the plants you are likely to see along the road as you walk to the island include bayberry, red cedar, swamp rows, and beach pea. You'll also have a wonderful view of the salt marsh, an interesting and relatively unique ecological habitat (there aren't many left), which is especially loved by birds. Snowy egrets, salt marsh sparrows, ducks, ospreys, and clapper rails (a secretive chickenlike bird that lives in the marsh ground) can be seen almost year-round. The island is also a great fall migration spot for a variety of other birds and some 100 different species stop here on their way south.

When you reach the island, the road splits in three. If you continue straight ahead, you'll pass through a stand of cedar and a grove of fruit trees, which date back to the 1800s when the area was farmland. If you're there in the fall, nominator Clay Taylor suggests you try a pear or an apple. Also in fall, monarch butterflies can be seen fluttering in the goldenrod on both sides of the path. They migrate just as the birds do, and hundreds of them stop by Willard's Island in September.

At the top of the hill, look for the fallen apple tree. The tree itself was blown down by Hurricane Gloria in 1985, but the roots are still embedded in the ground, and the tree still bears fruit. From here, there is a good view of the marsh and of Clinton Harbor, which was a big shipping port in the 1800s. "This is a nice place to be," Clay says. "You can scan the marsh for birds and look toward the harbor for boats."

At this point, the road forms a "T." If you go left or right, you'll see shrubs and bushes along the road, and you may spot some wildlife, such as a weasel or an owl. The stem of the T leads straight down to a dirt path which will take you to the marsh itself. Here you can see the estuaries, alive with crabs (it's a great place for crabbing) and a variety of fish. You will also see plant species, such as *spartina* grass, which are unique to the salt-marsh environment.

SOUTH CENTRAL CONNECTICUT

A Walking Tour of Yale

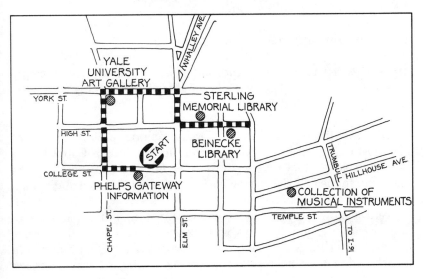

Directions: Yale University is located in New Haven. The walking tour of the campus begins at the Visitor Information Center, Phelps Gateway, 344 College Street. From Hartford, take I-91 south to exit 3 (Trumbull Street exit), and continue along Trumbull Street to the fourth traffic light. Turn left onto Prospect Street. After one block, Prospect Street becomes College Street. Drive for two and a half more blocks to the Visitor Information Office. From New York, take I-95 north to exit 47 (downtown New Haven), and continue to the first exit to the city streets. This will put you onto North Frontage Road. Drive for four blocks and turn right on York Street. Drive another four blocks to Elm Street and turn right. Continue for two blocks and turn right on College Street; Phelps Gateway is on the right in the middle of the block. Metered parking is available on College and Elm streets, and a large commercial garage is located on George Street between College and Temple streets.

Best Season: Year-round. Guided tours are given Monday through Friday at 10 a.m. and 2 p.m., and on Saturday and Sunday at 1:30 p.m. You can take a self-guided tour at any time by stopping at the Information Office for a copy of the *Walking Tour* pamphlet. For more information, call (203) 432-2300.

Length: 2½ miles. Allow about an hour.

Degree of Difficulty: Easy.

Highlights: Historic architecture and a visit to a rare book and manuscript library are just two of the highlights of this walking tour of the country's third-oldest university.

This walking tour of Yale University includes a view of some of the most unique buildings on the campus. The Phelps Gateway, the carved archway that houses the Visitor Information Center, marks the entry to the Old Campus, where Yale was established and named for Elihu Yale, a benefactor.

Yale is known throughout the world as an outstanding institution of higher learning, and this walk will take you past some of the reasons why. The Sterling Memorial Library, for example, the fourth-largest in the United States, contains 4 million books. During the academic year, the library is open Monday through Thursday, 8:30 a.m. to midnight; Friday and Saturday, 8:30 a.m. to 5 p.m.; and Sunday 1 p.m. to midnight. In the summer, the library is open Monday through Friday, 8:30 a.m. to 5 p.m., and Saturday 10 a.m. to 5 p.m.

Perhaps the most famous building on the tour is the Beinecke Rare Book and Manuscript Library, which is as beautiful a building on the outside as it is an important one on the inside. Its walls were designed with over 100 slabs of translucent marble, and the structure itself is an elegant combination of granite, bronze, and glass. Inside (the Beinecke is open from 8:30 a.m. to 5 p.m. Monday through Friday, and 10 a.m. to 5 p.m. on Saturday), there are numerous items of interest including ancient manuscripts and hand-printed books, a Gutenberg Bible, original bird prints by James Audubon, and letters from authors such as Mark Twain, Jack London, Ernest Hemingway, and Gertrude Stein.

Other important exhibitions are not included on the tour, but are popular attractions on campus, and well-worth visiting. The Yale University Art Gallery is the oldest university art museum in the western hemisphere; it contains numerous paintings by John Trumbull depicting scenes from the Revolutionary War period, as well as collections of Italian Renaissance paintings, pre-Columbian art and African sculpture, in addition to many other exhibits. The art gallery is open Tuesday through Saturday, 10 a.m. to 5 p.m., and Sunday, 2 to 5 p.m. The Yale Center for British Art is also open Tuesday through Saturday from 10 a.m. to 5 p.m., and Sunday from 2 to 5 p.m. The building, designed by Louis I. Kahn and opened to the public in 1977, houses the most comprehensive collection of English paintings, prints, drawings, rare books, and sculpture outside Great Britain.

The Peabody Museum of Natural History houses outstanding collections of fossils, featuring the great dinosaurs and a 110-foot-long *Age of Reptiles* mural that won a Pulitzer Prize. Hours are 9 a.m. to 4:45 p.m., Monday through Saturday, and Sunday from 1 to 4:45 p.m.

Those of you who are interested in music will not want to miss the Yale Collection of Musical Instruments on Hillhouse Avenue. It is open Tuesday through Thursday from 1 to 4 p.m. (closed every day during August), and Sunday from 2 to 5 p.m. (except during the summer months). Here you can inspect more than 800 musical instruments dating from the sixteenth century. Concerts are also performed here on a regular basis.

SOUTHEASTERN CONNECTICUT

Shoreline Walk in Waterford (13)

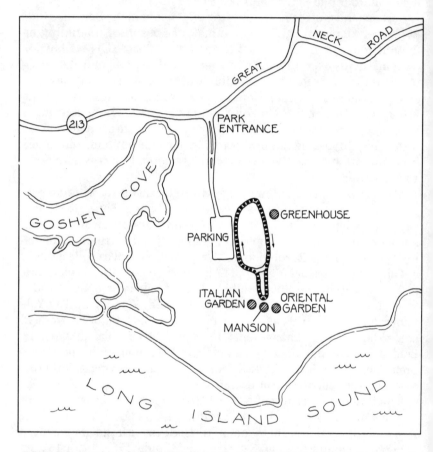

Directions: This walk is located in Harkness Memorial State Park, in Waterford, just south of New London. From I-95, take exit 75, and follow signs to the park.

Best Season: Spring and fall; the grounds are open year-round from 8 a.m. to sunset; buildings are open from 10 a.m. to 5 p.m. daily, Memorial Day through Labor Day.

Length: The park encompasses 125 acres; the shoreline walk is about 1 mile.

Degree of Difficulty: Easy.

Highlights: Beautiful gardens and nearly a mile of natural beach and salt marsh provide an inspiring place to enjoy the out-of-doors.

The Harkness Memorial State Park sits on Goshen Point, a rocky promontory near the confluence of the Thames River and Long Island Sound. It was on this scenic spit of land that the Edward S. Harkness Family built their summer estate, which they called Eolia. Both Edward Harkness (heir to his father's investments in John D. Rockefeller's Standard Oil) and his wife, Mary Stillman Harkness, shared a love of people and a feeling of responsibility toward society. Mr. Harkness bestowed over $200 million upon wide-ranging philanthropies. Mrs. Harkness gave generously to local organizations. She also was deeply concerned and touched by the difficulties of the handicapped, and in her will she provided for an ongoing rehabilitation and recuperation program to be carried out by the State of Connecticut. Before her death in 1950, she bequeathed the entire 234-acre estate to the people of Connecticut "to be used in a manner beneficial to public health." Half the park has been set aside as an exclusive recreation site for Connecticut's handicapped.

When Susan Morgan, who told us about this walk, visits the park, she likes to take a walk along the beach first. No swimming is allowed, but there are picnic areas, and fishing is permitted. There's an outdoor amphitheater on the grounds of the estate. "Many people get married there," Susan says. "You may see a bride and groom as you're walking along the beach!" Sailboats and ships can be seen on the sound and, of course, the ever-present sea gulls. It gets a little rocky around the fishing area, but all in all, this is an easy, pleasant stroll along the shore.

On the return trip, you'll see the back of the forty-two-room Italianate mansion, covered with vines and surrounded by gardens. (The mansion is currently undergoing renovation.) After your walk on the beach, Susan suggests you visit the gardens, which are at their peak during the last two weeks of July and the first two weeks of August. West of the main house are formal gardens designed in a Southern Mediterranean style with a central pool of water lilies, tall reeds, and water iris. Broad graveled pathways lined with clipped hedges lead to a U-shaped pergola, which is covered with wisteria and fox grapes. The cryptomeria tree growing near the pergola was a gift from the people of Japan in appreciation of the generosity of the Harknesses.

The Oriental Garden to the east of the mansion provides an interesting contrast, with urns, exotic statuary, and heavily perfumed plants from Asia. Wildflower displays, rock gardens, dogwoods, pine trees, and cedars add to the beauty of this very peaceful, picturesque scene.

Beyond the dog cemetery are a garage and chauffeur's quarters, and beyond that a greenhouse, where seedling stock is grown for the gardens.

SOUTHEASTERN CONNECTICUT

New London: Ocean Beach Park Boardwalk (14)

Directions: Driving north on I-95, take exit 75; driving south on I-95, take exit 83S. From the exits, all roads are marked to Ocean Beach Park.

Best Season: Spring and fall; winter is also good because it is less crowded.

Length: The boardwalk is ⅓ mile, but there are numerous places to walk in the park and lots to see. Allow at least one to two hours for minimal enjoyment.

Degree of Difficulty: Easy.

Highlights: This enjoyable walk combines panoramic scenery with good fellowship and a host of waterfront activities.

"A walk in Ocean Beach Park is both an exhilarating and calming experience," explains nominator Eleanor Butler. "It allows one to have a personal touch with nature at its best—open sky, ocean, waterfowl, birds—while being surrounded by the bustling activities of the waterfront: fishing boats, tugboats, submarines, sailboats, tankers, freighters, and ferryboats."

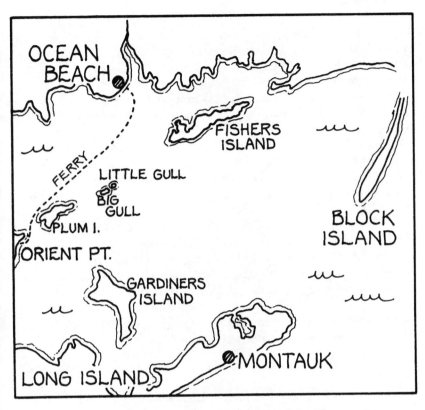

Ocean Beach Park is located at the mouth of the Thames River, on one of the most panoramic sections of Long Island Sound. There are views of Fishers Island, Little Gull and Big Gull islands, and Gardiners Island. On particularly clear days you can even see Montauk Point on the eastern tip of Long Island.

The human activities along this little piece of waterfront are fascinating. "Throughout the day, ferries can be seen merrily steaming by the beachfront on their way to Block Island or Orient Point," Eleanor says. "At times, you'll see submarines of all makes and classes heading out to the open sea from the U.S. Submarine Base. Other navigable delights include the U.S. Coast Guard's bark, *Eagle*, off-sounding sailboat races, tankers and freighters heading to the State Pier in New London, and fishing dories heading out to Race Rock for the best "catch of the day."

There are many places to walk in the park which provide a variety of surfaces and sights. Eleanor says the most popular walking spot is the boardwalk which fronts a beautiful white, sandy beach. Here you'll find fast-paced striders and leisurely strollers. The more adventuresome can scale rough-faced rocks at the west end of the beach; everyone can enjoy the flower-bedecked paths along the east end's miniature golf area.

Eleanor sent us an evocative description of this walk which we would like to share with you: "Various fowl can be seen with the changing seasons and nesting habits. Sea gulls and terns fly almost continuously overhead, scavenging their daily rations. Osprey, an endangered species, refortify their nests in the towers of the boardwalk and parking lot to ensure the safety of their young. A lordly duck assumes his sole ownership of the pool after the evening's summer crowd has left for the day. Flocks of pigeons join in the springtime scatterings of popcorn. And the sudden surge of great flocks of geese heading north or south portends the change of season.

"The intermittent sounds of foghorns and tugboat whistles do not intrude on the sounds of nature; rather they add a picturesque touch to the sense of scenic vastness that greets the eye. Lofty clouds, sometimes snow-white and feathery, sometimes heavy and black like smoke, span the horizon much like a rainbow, adding dimension to the uniqueness of the park's daily show."

SOUTHEASTERN CONNECTICUT

Fort Griswold (15)

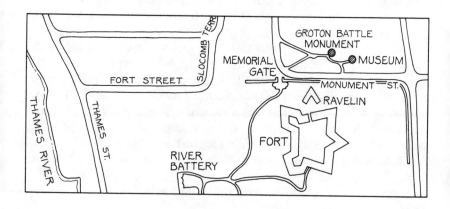

Directions: Fort Griswold is located in Fort Griswold State Park, across the Thames River from New London in Groton, Connecticut. From I-95, take exit 87 and follow signs to the fort.

Best Season: The park is open year-round from 8 a.m. to sunset. The Monument House Museum is open daily from Memorial Day through Labor Day, 9 a.m. to 5 p.m., and from Labor Day through Columbus Day on weekends, 9 a.m. to 5 p.m.

Length: The park encompasses some 17 acres; allow about three hours.

Degree of Difficulty: Easy.

Highlights: This historic walk takes you back to 1781 and the Battle of Groton Heights during which the British led 800 men against 150 Americans at Fort Griswold.

Before exploring the fort itself, nominator Jonathan Lincoln suggests you stop at the Groton Battle Monument and Museum where Revolutionary War artifacts and exhibits will help put you in the mood for this walk back into America's early history. The 134-foot granite monument is dedicated to the men who defended Fort Griswold during the Battle of Groton Heights in September 1781. As you walk through the fort and learn about the history of this battle, keep the date in mind: Just one month later, General Cornwallis surrendered at Yorktown, and the fighting was over.

During the revolution, New London was a thorn in the side of the British because it was home port to many privately owned armed ships, licensed by the State of Connecticut, whose owners took particular pride in capturing British ships. New London itself was poorly protected by the unfinished Fort Trumbull, but across the Thames River on Groton Heights stood Fort Griswold—ready and fortified.

So, in late summer 1781, when the British, hoping to distract Washington from his march south and at the same time revenge the capture of British ships, attacked New London under the direction of Benedict Arnold (who had deserted the American cause the year before), New Londoners had no choice but to flee. But on the other side of the river, 150 militia and local men led by Colonel William Ledyard, who expected reinforcements at any moment, stood fast as 800 British, under command of Colonel Eyre, marched on the fort. When Colonel Eyre demanded surrender, Colonel Ledyard refused. However, his 150 men were no match for the disciplined British troops, and eventually he was forced to submit. Details of what happened next are in dispute. American accounts state that when Ledyard surrendered, he was murdered with his own sword by the British, who then unleashed a massacre against the remaining Americans. British accounts make no mention of this.

Wounded American soldiers were taken to Ebenezer Avery's house, which at that time was on Thames Street. In 1971, the house was moved to its present location near the fort; it is open to the public from June through August, on weekends only from 1 to 5 p.m.

After your tour of Fort Griswold, plan a visit to Groton, home of America's submarine fleet and the USS *Nautilus* Submarine Force Museum.

SOUTHEASTERN CONNECTICUT

A Walking Tour of Norwich (16)

Directions: Take Route 395 to exit 81 east. At the stop sign, turn right. Continue through two traffic lights and park.

Best Season: Summer and fall.

Length: About 3 miles, or one hour—without stopping.

Degree of Difficulty: Easy.

Highlights: Fascinating old homes, a rose garden, a zoo, and "maybe even a brass band," says nominator Beryl Fishbone, are part of this walk through historic Norwich.

This walking tour is a brief introduction to the architectural variety of Norwich as well as a glimpse at the town's past.

Start on Rockwell Street where two homes, No. 42, built in 1818, and No. 44, built in 1750, are open to the public. Farther up Rockwell,

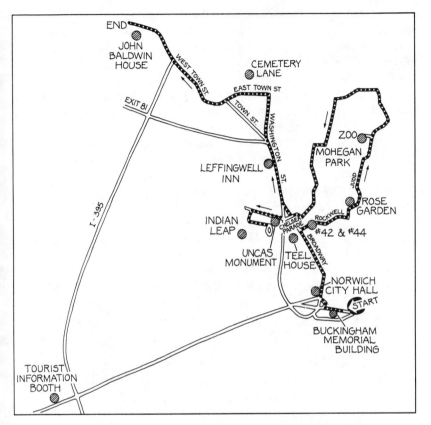

where it meets Judd Street, is a memorial rose garden, dedicated to Norwich veterans of World War II. There are more than 2,500 plants in this two-acre garden, and a festival is held every summer when the roses are in full glorious bloom. The rose has had special significance to the residents of Norwich ever since Henry Ward Beecher called the town the "Rose of New England."

Continue along Judd to Mohegan Park, 350 acres of hiking trails, picnic and swimming areas, and a children's zoo. If your time is limited, you may want to spend the rest of it right here, hiking in the park. You can then walk back to your car the way you came. However, there are a few more sites in Norwich that shouldn't be missed.

The Old Leffingwell Inn, at 348 Washington Street, for example. Open for tours to the public, the inn was built as a small house in 1675 by

Stephen Backus. Thomas Leffingwell enlarged it and received permission to "keep a publicque house for entertainment for strangers."

For cemetery aficionados, there's a dandy at 40 East Town Street (Cemetery Lane). Opened in 1714, among its "residents" are the remains of twenty French soldiers killed during the Revolutionary War.

Indians, of course, were the first residents of Connecticut (the name comes from the Indian word *Quinnehtukqut*, which means "beside the long tidal river"). Uncas Monument on Sachem Street marks the site of a Royal Indian Burial Ground, and Indian Leap (Yantic Falls) on Yantic Street is so-named because the Narragansetts fled by the spot with the Mohegans in hot pursuit after the Battle of East Great Plains in 1643.

At Broadway and Washington streets is an area called Chelsea Parade, which was deeded to the town by three of its citizens and first used (in 1792) as a place to review the 20th Regiment of the Infantry. At 9 Chelsea Parade South is Teel House. Built in 1789 as an inn, it is thought that George Washington danced in the third-floor ballroom.

Before you leave Norwich, nominator Beryl Fishbone especially recommends a visit to the John Baldwin House at 210 West Town Street. Built in 1660 by the founder of Norwich, it is open to the public and features hearth baking and weaving demonstrations.

SOUTHEASTERN CONNECTICUT

Stonington Borough (17)

Directions: Take exit 91 off I-95, and follow signs to Stonington Village, 2½ miles south.

Best Season: Spring through fall.

Length: About 1 mile, but there's lots to see and do. Allow at least a half a day.

Degree of Difficulty: Easy.

Highlights: A picturesque seaside village with historic buildings and homes that reflect a panorama of New England architecture, interesting shops, a lighthouse museum, "eighteen-pounder" cannons, and fantastic views of Rhode Island and New York from Stonington Point.

Stonington, one of the most picturesque of all Connecticut seaside communities, has a rich history, first as an eighteenth-century fishing and coastal trading village, then as a profitable shipbuilding, sealing, and whaling center in the nineteenth century. Today this history is preserved and can be seen firsthand on this walk submitted by Harriett Bessette.

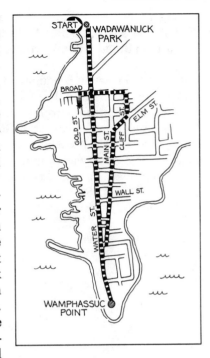

The walk begins in Wadawanuck Park and follows Water Street to its end at Stonington Point. As you pass the early frame homes on Water Street, note that many have been set up on brick bases so that their doors, once on street level, are now up one floor. Just past Wall Street, you'll see the former Ocean Bank, a Greek Revival building which is still used as a bank. Inside you can see the historic sixteen-star, sixteen-bar flag that was created in 1796 by the women of the Congregational Church to honor Tennessee as the sixteenth state. The flag flew proudly at the Battle of Stonington in the War of 1812. Across from the bank are two "eighteen-pounder" cannons which the local militia used to repulse a British naval attack in August 1814.

As you continue along Water Street, you'll come to an octagonal-towered lighthouse which serves as a museum operated by the Stonington Historical Society. The original lighthouse was built in 1823 and was the first in Connecticut. It was moved to higher ground in 1840.

From Stonington Point at the end of Water Street, there is a wonderful view across the water to Watch Hill, Rhode Island, and to Fishers Island, New York. Spend as much time as you want here, then head back via Main Street. At the corner of Ash and Main is the cottage of ropemaker Thomas Ash, built in 1790. Several other old homes line Main Street, including the Amos Palmer House, which was built in 1780. James McNeill Whistler lived here as a child and later the house was owned by Stephen Vincent Benet.

When you get to Elm Street, take a left to Cliff Street and climb "Sal Tinker's Hill," which leads through an alley to Broad Street. A left turn on Broad will take you back to Main Street and Wadawanuck Park.

Now head west on Broad Street toward the harbor. Robinson Burying Ground lies behind the high stone wall. Turn left onto Gold Street (so-named because a jeweler's shop was in one of the orange-brick homes you see at the corner of Gold and High), then right down the hill to the Town Dock where the lobster boats and fishing trawls are moored. The dock was originally built for the steamboats which arrived from New York and connected with the Stonington and Providence Railroad. Stop here to witness the activity in Stonington Harbor and to contemplate a maritime heritage that continues to this day.

SOUTHERN MAINE

Kennebunkport (18)

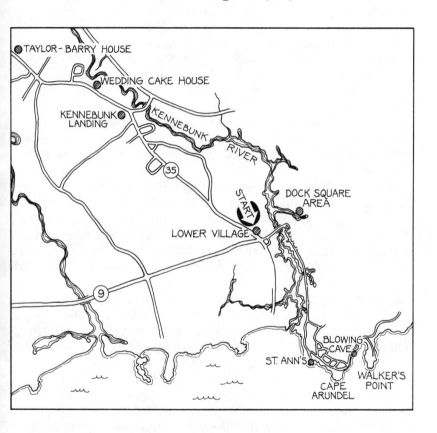

Directions: Take the Maine Turnpike to exit 3. Follow Route 35 east, to Route 9, to Dock Square. Turn right on Ocean Avenue. There's a parking area just beyond the Breakwater Inn.

Best Season: Spring through late fall, but, according to one of the nominators, Mary Folsom, winter is also nice, because it's quiet.

Length: 3 to 5 miles.

Degree of Difficulty: Moderate.

Highlights: A walk along the coast of Maine. "It's just breathtaking," says the other nominator, Bob Ellis.

If the meandering 2,800 miles of Maine's spectacular shoreline were to be rearranged in a straight line, the total would be reduced, incredibly, to just 230 miles. This gives you some idea of the extent and complexity of the hundreds of little coves and harbors that sprinkle the coast from Passamaquoddy Bay in the north to Kittery Point in the south. One of the most picturesque of all these little harbors is that of Kennebunkport, and this walk along Ocean Avenue is, according to Bob Ellis, "one of the most beautiful places in all of New England."

As you walk in the fresh sea air with the seabirds soaring overhead, be sure to notice the lobster boats. Watching them from the shore, you get the feeling that a picture postcard has come to life, and you sense the quintessence of the state of Maine, where 80 to 90 percent of the country's lobsters are caught. This delicacy, every bit as popular today as it was back when the native Indians alone loved it, is in short supply, both from the large demand for it and from damage inflicted by oil spills. In Maine, only residents are allowed to catch lobsters in state waters and then only older lobsters—those at least 3³⁄₁₆ inches long. Perhaps it would be a good idea if we, as a country, declared a two- to five-year-long moratorium on the eating of lobsters to allow this crustacean treasure to get back on its "feet."

In addition to the views in and above the water, this walk also affords a glimpse at some interesting land sites as well; the summerhouse of George Bush, for example, called Walker's Point; a picturesque New England church, St. Ann's, which was built in 1887 of sea rocks from the area and which includes stained-glass windows of seashells; and the Haunted House, home to many a mystery series, where filming takes place on the high cliffs. There are also a number of art galleries, numerous charming shops in Arundel Court, and the old homes of merchants and sea captains, many of which have been designated as "historic zones."

Mary Folsom suggests you take a walk down among the rocks when the tide is low. But she urges caution. "These rocks are slippery," she says, "and since many are smooth and well-rounded, there is no firm grip under foot."

Bob Ellis sent us this nomination because he wanted to share his memorable walk in Kennebunkport with others. "I have never entered a contest," he told us, "or even considered writing to a newspaper or magazine. But when I heard about nominations for the 'Best Walk,' I couldn't be silent. There is no place more beautiful than Kennebunkport!"

SOUTHERN MAINE

Portland: Uptown Art Walk (19)

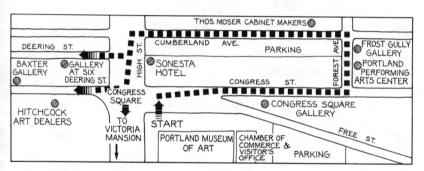

Directions: Take exit 8 from the Maine Turnpike, and stop at the Portland Museum of Art or the Congress Square Gallery (or any other "Art Walk" location) to pick up a brochure.

Best Season: Summer.

Length: 1½ miles. Allow about two hours or more, depending on your personal interests.

Degree of Difficulty: Easy.

Highlights: A collection of galleries, museums, the old "Victoria Mansion" and the Thos. Moser Cabinet Makers are all a part of this unique walk.

John Marin, Edward Hopper, Winslow Homer, and Andrew Wyeth are just a few of the Maine artists who have made this state such an important contributor to the heritage and vitality of American art. Now, on this very unusual and fascinating walk, designated throughout by a *blue line*, the walker has an opportunity to get an up-close look at art by artists from Maine. In the words of the nominator of this walk, it provides a "discovery opportunity to explore Portland [and all of Maine] from the perspective of its arts."

The association of Portland with Maine's artistic activities is a long one, dating back to the early 1800s when the Portland Society of Art was formed by a group of business people and artists. The formation of this society led to the founding of the Portland School of Art and the Portland Museum of Art. This walk, a tribute to Portland and to the artists of Maine, was a privately funded project that was given as a gift to the city by local business people.

The walk begins at the Portland Museum of Art, located at Seven Congress Square. In addition to numerous Maine artists, the museum—an award-winning building designed by architect I. M. Pei—also houses centuries of fine examples of American and European Art. At 594 Congress Street there's the Congress Square Gallery, where you'll find a collection of works by contemporary Maine artists, as well as traditional fine-art limited editions and Japanese woodblock prints. The Frost Gully Gallery at 25 Forest Avenue is home to paintings, drawings, prints, and sculpture by contemporary Maine artists.

From an historical perspective, one of the most interesting stops is the Thos. Moser Cabinet Makers at 415 Cumberland Avenue. Here you can see woodworking artistry that goes back to the eighteenth century. Modern technology now combines with traditional methods to create furniture of lasting beauty and quality.

Stop by the lobby of the Sonesta Hotel at 157 High Street for a look at the work of some well-known Maine artists, and then cross the street to Baxter Gallery, part of the Portland School of Art, at 619 Congress, where you'll find exhibits of contemporary art and photography as well as the school's art library, the finest in northern New England. If you see an artist you are particularly interested in, Hitchcock Art Dealers at 602 Congress offers a wide variety of works by contemporary Maine artists.

Just off the blue-line Art Walk, on Danforth Street, is the Victoria Mansion. One of the finest examples of nineteenth-century eclectic architecture to survive in the United States, this "Italian villa" brownstone, with its opulent interior and original furnishings, is well-worth a visit. It is open to the public from June through September.

Plan time for a leisurely lunch sometime during your walk at one of the many restaurants along the way. There's everything from Chinese, American, and Continental cuisine to the "World's Greatest Hamburgers" and specialties from Afghanistan.

Most of the galleries are open Monday through Friday, but there are special evening and weekend hours. The Portland Museum of Art is closed on Monday. For additional information, contact the Portland Chamber of Commerce at (207) 772-2811.

Just outside Portland, a little way north on I-95, is the "Desert of Maine," an anomaly in the heavily wooded "Pine Tree State." Plan to visit this dune-filled place which was once a farm. Overcutting and overgrazing caused the thin layer of topsoil to erode, and dunes were created when the underlying glacial deposits of sand were blown by the wind. A visit here makes a nice contrast to your city art tour.

SOUTHERN MAINE

Old Orchard Beach (20)

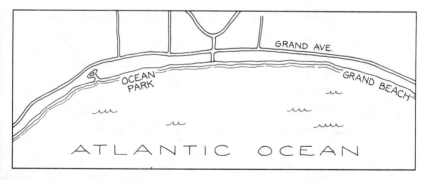

Directions: From Portland, take I-95 (Maine Turnpike) south to exit 5. Follow signs to Old Orchard Beach.

Best Season: May through October, but it's good all year.

Length: 14 miles round-trip.

Degree of Difficulty: Easy; flat, hard surface on low-tide sand.

Highlights: A walk on the "most beautiful beach in the world!"

This is a refreshing easy walk which can clear the mind and exhilarate the spirit year-round. Nominator Beverly Meltzer-Boxtein likes to walk it barefoot, and she recommends you try it that way— but not in the colder months. "It's better to wear sneakers then," she says. The "low-tide" sand provides just the right surface for walking without getting tired.

The ocean forms a gentle curve into the silver-white sandy beach at this 7-mile stretch, and during the summer it's fun to run in and out of the water or just watch the vacationers and local residents enjoying themselves on the beach or sitting under the shade of their umbrellas.

Behind the sea walls opposite the ocean side, primly beautiful summer cottages look out over the Atlantic. ("Rose Kennedy's family used to summer here," Beverly says). Alongside these historic homes are new condominiums, beautiful in a more modern way and very "controlled." They are nicely spaced and not too tall. Beverly says that contractors are not allowed to build them any higher than seven stories.

The public beach enjoys an unusual low-tide depth of at least ¼-mile, which lasts for hours. Beverly calls it a "fresh-air wonder of the world." Sea gulls soar overhead as children run along the beach collecting seashells and rare stones, darting into the water every now and then to cool their feet. Beverly loves the walk for its beauty and for the opportunity it affords to get exercise. "The scene is always changing," she says, "and it's a joy to breathe the wondrous air as you walk the most beautiful beach in the world!"

SOUTHERN MAINE

Crescent Beach (21)

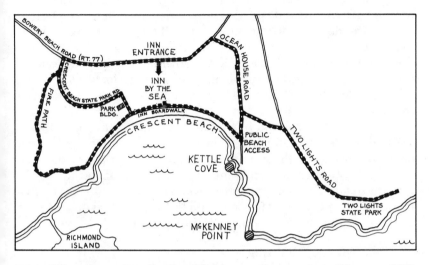

Directions: From Portland, take I-95 south to exit 7. Pleasant Hill Road connects to Route 77 (Bowery Beach Road) and leads to the Inn by the Sea, where you can meet David Costa, the concierge, who nominated this walk.

Best Season: Fall (September and October).

Length: 2 miles.

Degree of Difficulty: Moderate.

Highlights: "One of the most beautiful places on earth."

David Costa grew up near Crescent Beach, and he has never left the area—at least not permanently. "I see the sun sparkling on the water and the lobster boats silhouetted on the horizon. It never ceases to delight me." He nominated this walk to encourage others to experience the place for themselves.

The coves of Crescent Beach afford an opportunity to meet the captains of local fishing boats as they come in from a day's work. If they have time, they will share their enthusiasm for the sea with you and perhaps even some old "fish tales."

As you stroll southward along the beach, you'll notice the impressive Sprague Estate and Richmond Island, which separates Seal Cove from Saco Bay. Named for Irishman George Richmond, who settled here in 1620, Richmond Island is indeed rich, both in natural beauty and in legends. Its history abounds with tales of buried treasure and Indian lore.

Heading north, you'll pass by Kettle Cove and you'll see McKenney Point, an area that has been particularly treacherous for boats. In 1947, for example, the 300-foot coal steamer *Oakey L. Alexander* ran aground there and split in two.

Now the walk takes you in a westerly direction, through a lovely wooded place and then north where picturesque farms can be seen on your way back to the inn. Here, along Route 77, David tells us he greets the local postal carrier and chats with her about her hometown in Ireland, or the local grocer, who is a sports enthusiast. "I've met people from all over the world on this beach," David says. "It's because it's one of the most beautiful places on earth."

SOUTHERN MAINE

Mackworth Island Nature Walk (22)

Directions: From Route 1 in Falmouth, follow signs to the Mackworth Island Causeway.

Best Season: Spring and summer; there's cross-country skiing in winter.

Length: About 2 miles.

Degree of Difficulty: Easy.

Highlights: A beautiful walk on an island bird sanctuary.

Mackworth Island is connected to the mainland by a causeway. "For quite a few years it was a wooden bridge," says nominator Lorraine Hanson, "and before that you could reach the island only by sailing vessel." The island was donated to the state for use as a bird sanctuary and school for the deaf. Lorraine, who lives in nearby Falmouth, walks the perimeter of the island almost every day. She loves it for all the interesting things she sees and for the people she meets.

"In the spring and fall," she says, "we see geese—hundreds of them. And this year I have seen two white owls with a little gray on them. They stayed around the island for a couple of months. In the summer we take a lunch and stay for hours. I always look for interesting flowers like lady's slippers, but I'm not telling exactly where they are. People would pick them, and that would be the end of them."

Birds will follow you all along your walk on this beautiful island, and you'll have wonderful views of the water and the nearby islands of Chebeague, Long, and Peaks. And you'll meet some nice people, too.

"As I start my walk each day, I meet a lot of people," Lorraine says. "No celebrities, but just a lot of nice people. I have met people that I went to school with and haven't seen for years, and people who live as far away as California. Almost everyone thinks, as I do, that the walk is a beautiful one. My brother- and sister-in-law live in Atlanta, Georgia, and my other brother and his family live in Florida. Ever since I started taking them to Mackworth Island, they want to go back and walk it again every time they come to Maine."

SOUTHERN MAINE

Wolfe's Neck Woods: Shoreline Walk (23)

Directions: The walk is located in Wolfe's Neck Woods State Park, 4½ miles from downtown Freeport. From Route 1 in Freeport, take Bow Street (opposite L. L. Bean) south for 1⁶⁄₁₀ miles; bear right at the park sign, and drive ⁸⁄₁₀ mile to Wolfe's Neck Road. Turn right onto Wolfe's Neck Road, and go 2²⁄₁₀ miles to the park gate, which is on the left just beyond the field.

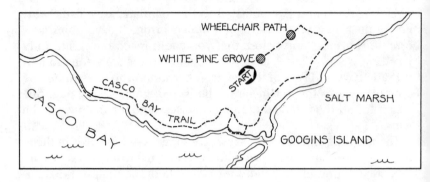

Best Season: Year-round.

Length: Approximately ¾ mile one way. Allow about an hour for a pleasant round-trip.

Degree of Difficulty: Easy.

Highlights: Cool sea breezes, views of the bay, and a chance to see a wide variety of waterfowl are some of the special features of this walk along Casco Bay.

Each season boasts its own special features on this beautiful walk along Casco Bay in Wolfe's Neck Woods State Park. In spring, the floor of the pine forest is dotted with colorful wildflowers; in summer great blue heron can be seen feeding in Little River Bay, a shallow part of Casco Bay; in late winter you can watch flocks of migrating ducks perform their courting rituals; in fall the foliage is breathtaking.

There are 5 miles of trail in Wolfe's Neck Woods, and three walk loops that are particularly popular; the Woods Walk is about 1.3 miles, the Park Loop Walk is about 1.8 miles, and the Shoreline Walk, which nominator Patricia Bailey particularly enjoys, follows the Wheelchair Path and the Casco Bay Trail for about ¾ mile.

Begin the walk near the end of the second parking lot, at the White Pine Grove, and follow the Wheelchair Path through the pine grove and picnic area to a four-way trail intersection. At this point, turn right, toward Casco Bay. Patricia says you can get a good view of the bay if you walk down the wooden stairway that leads to the salt marsh.

Continue along the path, following the bay to an overlook from which you can see Googins Island, an osprey sanctuary not open to the public. From mid-April to mid-September a pair of osprey nest on the island, and it is very important not to disturb the birds at this time. You may see other ospreys circling overhead, as the nesting couple will not allow them on the island! Ospreys are big birds, with wingspans ranging from five to six feet; they feed only on fish and are sometimes called the Fish Hawk. These birds were once endangered by pesticide poisoning and habitat loss, but ospreys are making a comeback, especially along the coast of Maine.

From the overlook, log steps lead down to the shore, where you can take a stone path to the rocks. "It's interesting to see what lives on this rocky shore," Patricia says. "You're likely to see barnacles, blue mussels, crab, periwinkles, and rockweeds." If you continue down the shore for about 100 feet, you'll come to a stone stairway which leads up to a four-way intersection. You can turn left, back onto the Casco Bay Trail, which affords beautiful views of the water, and continues for about ³⁄₁₀ mile. You may see cormorants, harbor ducks, or even see a harbor seal, and you're sure to catch a sea breeze. This is the coolest part of the entire park.

Wolfe's Neck State Park encompasses over 200 acres and was a gift to Maine from Mr. and Mrs. Lawrence M. C. Smith, of Freeport. It is believed that the area was originally settled in 1666 by Thomas and Anne Shepherd, whose granddaughter Rachel married Henry Woolf, the first long-time resident on the peninsula. He lived out his life here, and has been remembered in the name of Wolfe's Neck— with various spellings over time. Guided walks within the park are available year-round, and there are education programs headed by the park naturalist. For more information, call (207) 865-4465.

SOUTHERN MAINE

Wiscasset Harbor (24)

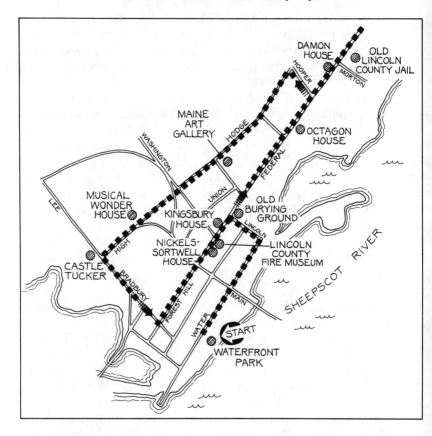

Directions: Wiscasset is located on the coast of southern Maine, just north of Bath on Highway 1. This walk begins at Waterfront Park, off Water Street on the Sheepscot River.

Best Season: June through September.

Length: 3 miles. Allow about half a day for a leisurely walk along the river in Wiscasset.

Degree of Difficulty: Easy.

Highlights: Wiscasset is a charming harbor town; this walk recalls its prosperous days as a thriving shipping center.

Adapted from the book *Walking Tours of New England,* by Kenneth Winchester and David Dunbar, this walk begins at Waterfront Park where you have a good view of two abandoned schooners, the *Hesper* and the *Luther Little,* the last of more than 500 four-masted schooners built in Maine. They are reminders of Wiscasset's prosperous days when its year-round harbor, one of Maine's deepest, made this town a port for the great sailing ships. Other reminders can be found in the fine old homes that many of the wealthy sea captains and shipping tycoons built in Wiscasset.

From Waterfront Park, follow Water Street past Main Street to Lincoln. Turn left on Lincoln, then right on Federal Street. At the corner of Lincoln and Federal, you'll see the Old Burying Ground, also known as the Ancient Cemetery, where the oldest tombstone dates back to 1739.

Continue down Federal Street past a number of old homes to the Octagon House on your right. Built in 1855, this is one of the few eight-sided structures in Maine. Just before Morton Street on your left is the Damon House, which was built in 1805. Just past Morton on your right is the Old Lincoln County Jail, the first penitentiary in Maine. The building was completed in 1811 and was used as a prison until 1954. The jailor's house was added in 1839 and now houses the Lincoln County Museum, which is open to the public Tuesday through Sunday from June to mid-September. Inside you'll find a tool exhibit and a number of displays.

Retrace your steps back down Federal Street and make a right on Hooper and a left on Hodge Street. Continue along Hodge to the Maine Art Gallery, where during the summer there are wonderful exhibits of Maine's foremost artists and sculptors.

Walk along Hodge Street, across Washington to Wiscasset's Green, one of the prettiest in Maine. A walk to the end of High Street will take you past a number of stately old homes, including the Musical Wonder House, an old sea captain's home which is now a museum (open in the summer) featuring mechanical musical instruments from the past 200 years. Here you can see a pipe organ from the nineteenth century, an 1812 Swiss music box, French musical dolls, and player pianos. Guided tours feature demonstrations of the instruments, and there is a shop where you can buy piano rolls and vintage sheet music.

At the end of High Street, cross over Lee for a visit to Castle Tucker. Open Tuesday through Saturday in July and August, Castle Tucker affords a wonderful view of Wiscasset's harbor from Windmill Hill. The unusual structure was built in 1807, at great cost, by Judge Silas Lee for his wife Tempe. Inside are the original Victorian furnishings of Captain Richard Tucker, who bought the house in 1857, and an intriguing "flying" staircase. You may also feel the presence of a ghost or two: The home is thought by some to be haunted.

From the "castle," follow Bradbury Street toward the river to Fort Hill and turn left. Walk down Fort Hill, past Main Street, to the Nickels-Sortwell House, a Federal structure with one of New England's "most beautiful doorways," according to photographer Samuel Chamberlain. The mansion, which is open Tuesday through Sunday from June to the end of October, is noted for its fireplaces and woodwork; the carving in the front hall took two years to complete. Now, walk down Federal Street, past the Kingsbury House on your left (built in 1763, this is the oldest two-story dwelling in Wiscasset) to Lincoln Street. A right on Lincoln and another right on Water Street will lead you back to Waterfront Park.

SOUTHERN MAINE

Historic Augusta (25)

Directions: This walking tour of Maine's capital city is divided into two parts, one on the east side of the Kennebec River, one on the west side. The East Tour begins at Fort Western on Cony Street, the West Tour begins at the State House on the corner of Capitol and State streets.

Best Season: Spring through fall.

Length: Each tour is about 2 miles and takes 2 to 3 hours.

Degree of Difficulty: Easy.

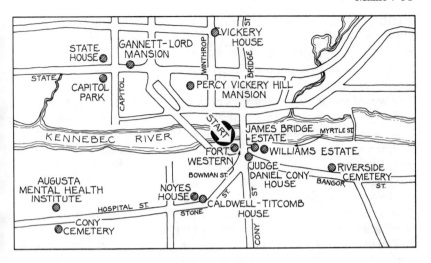

Highlights: By concentrating on the elegant buildings of the early eighteenth and nineteenth centuries, this walk gives you a glimpse of Maine's capital city at its richest and most powerful.

The Kennebec River divides Maine's capital in two, and this walking tour, nominated by Peter Marczak, is in two parts: the East Tour and the West Tour. We suggest you take one in the morning, stop for lunch, and take the other in the afternoon. Since Augusta's origins are on the east side, it might be appropriate to take the East Tour first. It begins at Fort Western on Cony Street.

Fort Western was a supply fort built by the British in 1754. Fifteen years later, Captain James Howard, the fort's first commander, bought it, along with about 900 surrounding acres, and set up a trading post. This was the beginning of Augusta. During the American Revolution and for many years afterward, political dignitaries were often entertained at the "Great House of Captain Howard," but by the 1900s, Fort Western was a forgotten shell of its former self. Then, in 1919, William Howard Gannett, one of Captain Howard's descendants, restored it to its original state and gave it to the city of Augusta. Today, from mid-May through August, the public can visit Fort Western and view eighteenth-century period rooms, collections of early military items, early tools, and Indian relics.

Across Cony Street from the fort, at 9 Myrtle Street, is the Williams

Estate—one of the buildings along the walk that nominator Peter Marczak likes best. It was built in the late eighteenth century and is an excellent example of the transitional period from the Federal style of architecture to the Greek Revival style. The house at 12 Myrtle Street once belonged to James Bridge and Sarah Bowdoin Williams. The two were popular members of Augusta society and entertained lavishly in this stately Colonial estate.

Cemetery aficionados will not want to miss Riverside Cemetery on Bangor Street, which contains the remains of some of Augusta's early settlers, as well as those of a number of Revolutionary War soldiers. Of interest, too, is the Cony Cemetery on Hospital Street (the old "Vassalboro Coach Road"), where you'll find several slate headstones of the late eighteenth and early nineteenth century. Note the angel and death signs and unusual epitaphs.

The brick mansion at 71–73 Cony Street was built for Judge Daniel Cony, who first came to Augusta in 1777 and practiced medicine here for many years before retiring to life as a devoted public servant. Judge Cony founded the Cony Free Female Academy in 1818 and aided in the chartering of Hallowell Academy and Bowdoin College. He was also instrumental in having the state capital moved from Portland to Augusta.

The Augusta Mental Health Institute on Hospital Street is worth noting for its beautiful grounds, which have been graded and landscaped to reflect the gardens of the State House and Capitol Park (on the West Side Tour). From the Institute, follow Hospital Street back to Stone Street for a look at two more elegant old homes. The Italianate-style Noyes House at 72 Stone Street was built in 1876 by Nathaniel Noyes, a well-known Augusta builder. Notice how the cupola on top of the low-pitched roof reflects the details of the house. The Caldwell-Titcomb House stands at 66 Stone Street. This New England Regional Gothic revival mansion was built for William Caldwell and Abigail Stone Caldwell, daughter of the Reverend Stone, whose home was originally on this site and for whom the street is named.

The West Side Tour begins at the State House, originally designed by Boston architect Charles Bulfinch but later remodeled and enlarged. Great care was taken in the remodeling to preserve the Bulfinch double-tiered front porch, which remains intact. The 14-acre Capitol Park which surrounds the State House is considered one of the most beautiful in the United States. Here wide expanses of green lawn are divided by stately elms; an arboretum at the east end of the park contains thousands of trees, shrubs, ferns, and wildflowers, as well as a mile-long landscaped trail.

The homes on this West Side tour also reflect the history of eighteenth- and nineteenth-century Augusta. The Gannett-Lord Mansion, for example, at 184 State Street, was built for Guy Patterson Gannett, son of William Howard Gannett, who had started a monthly magazine called *Comfort* in 1888 (and who later was responsible for restoring Fort Western). Guy went into the publishing business with his father and in the mid-1920s moved to Portland to head up the firm which today is the huge Gannett Publishing Group. Augusta became something of a publishing center in the late 1800s. Another early publisher lived in the city in a home at 89 Winthrop Street. This Italianate mansion was designed by architect Francis Herny Fassett in 1874 for the Honorable Peleg Orison Vickery, who during the Civil War had sent reports to the *Kennebec Journal* about life in the Third Regiment. After the war, Vickery worked at the *Journal*, before deciding to bring out his own monthly paper which he called *Vickery's Fireside Visitor*. Within two years, the paper had reached a nationwide circulation of 165,000. When Vickery's daughter, Lizzie Green, married Dr. John Fremont Hill, the Vickery and Hill Publishing Company was formed. The magnificent Georgian–Colonial Revival mansion at 125 State Street was owned by the son of Lizzie and John Hill, Percy Vickery Hill. The mansion contains twenty-five rooms and a third-floor ballroom which is lit by a crystal chandelier and silver sconces. The drawing-room fireplace is framed by delft tiles from Holland.

SOUTHERN MAINE

Hallowell: Maine's "Antique Capital" (26)

Directions: Hallowell is just south of Augusta, off I-95. This walk begins at Kennebec Row at the juncture of Water and Central streets.

Best Season: Summer and fall.

Length: 3 miles. There's a lot to see here, especially if you are an antique lover. Allow a full day.

Degree of Difficulty: Easy.

Highlights: Hallowell is a quaint New England town, with church spires and stately old homes, but for antique lovers there's much more—a chance to search for treasure in more than twenty antique shops!

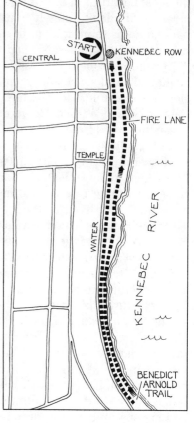

This walk, adapted from *Walking Tours of New England* by Kenneth Winchester and David Dunbar, follows Hallowell's Water Street from Kennebec Row at the end of Central Street to a bend in the Kennebec River known as "the hook." Along the way, you'll have an opportunity to sift through items from the past as you visit the numerous antique shops on Water Street. Many of these stores specialize in a particular item: doll houses and miniatures, for example, are the specialty of McLean Antiques: old stamps can be found at Howard's; and musical instruments, at Stephen Lapidus. There's a wonderful spirit of cooperation between store owners, so if you can't find what you're looking for in one place, just ask; it's sure to be somewhere on Water Street.

When you come to "the hook" you'll see the wooden signs that mark part of the Benedict Arnold Trail. In 1775, Arnold led 1,100 troops along this trail, en route to Quebec City, which he hoped to capture from the British. He and his men failed in their attempts, but they lay siege to the town until the British sent reinforcements. A wonderful view of Hallowell may help you reflect on these somewhat heady facts of history (Arnold, after all, turned traitor).

Retrace your steps along Water Street to Temple Street and turn right. There you can pick up a fire lane which makes a nice path along the Kennebec River back to Central Street and Kennebec Row, where the walk began. You'll find benches and picnic tables along the path which make a nice place to stop and relax or have a bite to eat.

NORTHEASTERN MAINE

QuaQuaJo Mountain Nature Walk (27)

Directions: QuaQuaJo Mountain is located in Aroostook State Park. Take I-95 to the Houlton exit (the last one before Canada). Turn left and follow Route 1 for about three-quarters of an hour. Watch for signs to the park, which is off to the left.

Best Season: Summer and fall.

Length: There are three trails on QuaQuaJo Mountain, ranging in length from ¾ mile to 1¼ miles. There is also a 4-mile cross-country ski trail which can be used for hiking in the summer.

Degree of Difficulty: Moderate to difficult.

Highlights: Beautiful views, scenic forests, and a variety of wildlife await you on QuaQuaJo Mountain.

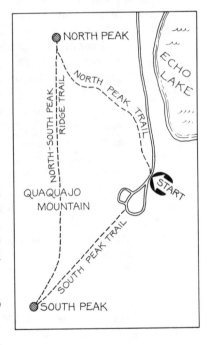

This walk on QuaQuaJo (pronounced QUAH-gy Jo) Mountain, the dominant feature in the more than 600-acre Aroostook State Park, is a wonderful sampling of the North Maine Woods, with forests of spruce, balsam fir, beech, and maple, as well as younger stands of poplar, birch, and other hardwoods. QuaQuaJo gets its name from the Indian word for the mountain, *QuaQuajo*, most popularly translated as "twin-peaked."

Nominator Ellen Schneider likes to combine the three trails on QuaQuaJo to make a loop of about 3 miles. Begin on the North Peak Trail, which starts at the day-use parking area and affords scenic views as you pass through forests of upland hardwoods and conifers. Squirrels, rabbits, chipmunks, deer, raccoons, and skunks are most frequently seen on the mountain trails, and, if you're lucky, you might also spot a fox, moose, bobcat, coyote, or even a black bear. There are many birds in the area, including owls, ruffed grouse, shorebirds, and a variety of songbirds.

After walking for about ¾ mile, you'll come to some large rocks which make a great place to sit and enjoy the view of beautiful Echo Lake at the eastern base of QuaQuaJo. At one time a brook flowed there; the lake was formed in the 1860s when a dam was built at the northern end of the brook to power a local saw mill. After your walk on the mountain, you can stop by Echo Lake for a swim and a picnic lunch. Fishing and boating are also popular on the lake.

From the rocks, continue on up to North Peak where you'll find more beautiful views of the surrounding farmlands. "It's especially beautiful at dusk," Ellen says. "The sunsets are gorgeous." The foliage is sparser on the peak because of the wind, but there are some hardy blueberry patches.

From North Peak, walk along the North-South Peak Ridge Trail, which meanders along the ridge between the two peaks for about 1 mile to South Peak. From here you can take the rugged ¾-mile South Peak Trail down to a campground which has thirty campsites, designed for tent or trailer camping. There are also two larger campsites available by reservation. For more information, call (207) 768-8341.

THE CENTRAL COAST

Bar Harbor Shore Path (28)

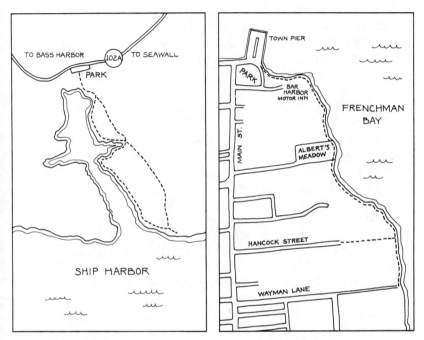

Directions: From Bangor, take Route 1-A to Ellsworth, where you pick up Route 3 to Bar Harbor.

Best Season: Summer and fall.

Length: About 1 mile.

Degree of Difficulty: Easy.

Highlights: Dazzling ocean views from a pathway that was once the promenade of the rich and powerful.

This walk, nominated by Earl Brechlin, begins at the Bar Harbor town pier near the boat launching ramp, just above the town beach.

From here you can take a boat tour to the nearby islands. A park near the pier provides a great place to sit and gaze out over the bay at Porcupine Islands and Schoodic Point on the mainland to the east.

The Shore Path leads from the pier to another park, called Albert's Meadow. Open to the public, this is a wonderful spot to enjoy a picnic lunch before continuing your walk past the former summer "cottages" of the wealthy. In the distant water, you'll see the lobster boats pulling their traps while seabirds soar overhead. Occasionally porpoise can be spotted. Stop to explore the numerous tide pools along the way, but try not to disturb anything. Tide pools are one of nature's most delicately balanced miracles.

About midway along the path is the Bar Harbor breakwater, where you can frequently see bald eagles. From here you can take a connecting path, marked by a board fence, to Hancock Street and on into the town of Bar Harbor, or continue walking a little farther to Wayman Lane which will also take you back into town.

Sharing Mount Desert Island with Bar Harbor is Acadia National Park, which combines spectacular ocean and mountain scenery in over 40 square miles. A 20-mile scenic drive through the park affords magnificent views and, for the walker, there are endless carriage roads and footpaths, including a challenging climb to the highest point on the east coast—the summit of Cadillac Mountain.

Before you tackle Cadillac Mountain, you might want to warm up with an easy hike on the Ship Harbor Nature Trail, and acquaint yourself with the natural wonders of Acadia National Park. This 1½-mile trail, made up of two loops, begins at the Seawall Campground parking lot and ends at the ocean, where you'll be rewarded with beautiful views of the Duck Islands. The trees and plant life on the trail are labeled to educate visitors about the vegetation indigenous to the park.

Nominator Earl Brechlin, a resident of Bar Harbor, has hiked in this area for more than fifteen years. Based on his experience and love of both the area and hiking, he has compiled a pocket hiking guide called *Twelve Walks on Mount Desert Island*. Both the Bar Harbor Shore Path and the hike up Cadillac Mountain are included in this little book as well as a variety of other walks designed to give a sampling of the more than 50 miles of carriage paths and 142 miles of trails in Acadia National Park. It's a perfect introduction to the area.

THE CENTRAL COAST

Deer Isle: A Walk in Stonington (29)

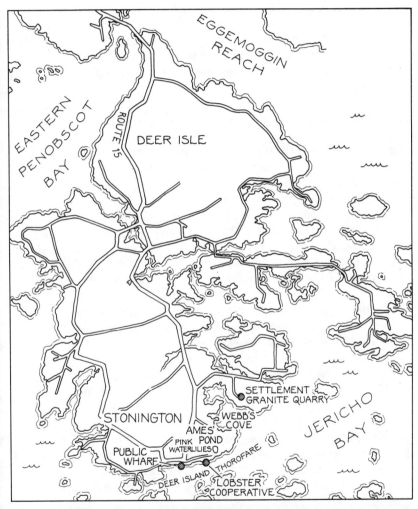

Directions: From Augusta, take Route 3 east to Belfast; from Portland, take Route 1 northeast to Belfast. Once in Belfast, continue northeast on Routes 1 and 3 to Bucksport. Follow Routes 1 and 3 through Bucksport to Route 15 south. Continue on 15, across a magnificent suspension bridge to Deer Isle and Stonington, which is on the southern tip of the island. You can park in the town of Stonington, at the end of Route 15.

Best Season: Year-round.

Length: 1½ miles round-trip, but you'll want to allow at least half a day for a visit to Deer Isle; more, if you decide to take a boat trip to Isle au Haut, where miles of walking trails wind through woods, along cliffs and on sandy beaches.

Degree of Difficulty: Moderately easy; there is one incline.

Highlights: This walk through the working fishing village of Stonington and along Stonington Harbor leads to a beautiful lily pond, one of the few in Maine.

Johanna G. Sherwood, President of the Deer Isle–Stonington Chamber of Commerce, nominated this walk to the lily pond in Stonington. It begins on Main Street. Walk east from the parking area, along Route 15, and take a right on Indian Point Road (the water—dotted with numerous coves, inlets, and islands—will be on your right), and you'll pass the Lobster Cooperative where the lobster boat captains bring their precious cargo. Along the way, you'll see the docks, in all probability piled high with lobster traps, and the brightly colored lobster-trap buoys decorate nearly every home, hanging on posts, on nails, and on the sides of barns. Don't be surprised if a seal pops up out of the water to greet you. Sea gulls perch on top of cottages and on the fish factory building, adding to the picturesque charm of Stonington.

Continue along the road by the shore to Ames' Pond, a lovely lily pond with pink lilies floating along its surface. You'll see frogs (or at least hear them) and often there are blue herons and other waterfowl along the edge of the water. "This is a leisurely walk," Johanna says, "and it gives you a chance to see what an active fishing village is like."

Stonington gets its name from the quality stone quarries that were developed there around 1870 and caused a "granite boom" that lasted from about 1885 to 1925. At its height, the town had some 3,500 inhabitants and enjoyed a prosperity that seemed destined to go on forever. Some of the structures made with granite from this area include the Brooklyn, Triborough, George Washington, and Manhattan bridges; the buildings in Rockefeller Center; the New York County Court House; and the John F. Kennedy Memorial at Arlington National Cemetery. Demand for the stone, however, did not last forever, and for a while some thought the industry would disappear. Those who despaired were far too pessimistic however; for, although demand for Deer Isle stone has not recovered to its peak by any means, it nevertheless is now on the increase. Stonington itself, perfectly content in its other roles as a fishing village and home to numerous artists and craftspeople, seems oblivious to the ups and downs of its famous industry (the largest working quarry is on Crotch Island in Stonington Harbor; there are two smaller working granite quarries in the town).

To get a different perspective on Deer Isle and the many nearby islands, there's nothing like a boat ride. You can take an excursion around the islands or a boat to Isle au Haut, a wooded 18-square-mile island where some 3,000 acres are part of Acadia National Park. Here you can walk for miles and miles through wooded areas, up on cliffs, along lakeshores, and on beautiful sandy beaches. Palmer Day IV Excursions have a 16-mile cruise that leaves from Stonington at 2 p.m. every day from July 4 through September 1. For more information, call (207) 376-2207. The Isle au Haut Boat Company operates the *Miss Lizzie*, which will take you out on a tour of the islands or on a round-trip to Isle au Haut from June to September. Call (207) 348-6038 for information about schedules and fares.

THE CENTRAL COAST

Main Street, Rockland (30)

Directions: Rockland is located off Route 1 at the center of midcoast Maine. This walk begins at the corner of Winter and Main streets, known as the Burpee and Singhi Block.

Best Season: Year-round.

Length: The walk is just four blocks, but Rockland is an interesting and picturesque place. You'll want to spend quite a bit of time here.

Degree of Difficulty: Easy.

Highlights: This walk includes a lighthouse museum and a stroll through Rockland's historic district which boasts a wide variety of architectural styles and buildings some 200 years old.

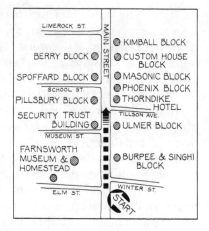

Rockland got a good start when Isaiah Tomlin arrived from Massachusetts in 1765 because Tomlin had twenty-one children, thus starting his own small population boom! At that time Rockland was known as Shore Village. Later the name was changed to Rockland because of the abundance of lime rock in the area. The population continued to increase when John Lermond and his brothers set up a logging camp. Before long, the town became a prominent port, and the shipbuilding and fishing industries thrived. Rockland also became an important center for retail shopping. On this tour of Main Street, you'll have a chance to browse through some of Rockland's shops, housed in buildings some 200 years old.

Rockland's Main Street historic district begins at the corner of Winter and Main streets at the pre-1858 Italianate structure of brick with wood trim known as the Burpee and Singhi Block. Next to this building is the Ulmer Block, built in 1858, also in the Italianate style. Across the street is the Security Trust Building, built in 1912, in the Colonial Revival style. Next door is the Pillsbury Block. This building, constructed in 1859, currently houses a department store, but it has been home to a number of different businesses as well as a college, county offices, and court rooms.

Cross the street for a close look at the Thorndike Hotel, which opened in 1855. Three more nineteenth-century Italianate business blocks, the Phoenix, Masonic, and Custom House, are next to the Thorndike. If you cross Main Street again, you can browse though the renovated Coffin's Clothing Store in the Spoffard Block. This building is on the site of Rockland's first cabin, dating from 1769. Next to Coffin's is the Berry Block, a Greek Revival building constructed by the Berry brothers during 1853 and 1854. The building next to this one was also built by the Berry brothers and was home to Gregory's Clothing Store for many years; now it's the Specialty Shop, a store featuring women's and children's clothing. It used to house the Limerock Bank, where a bungled bank robbery once took place.

The Kimball Block is on the corner of Maine and Limerock streets and was once a great commercial block. It was constructed in 1848 for Iddo Kimball, a prominent business, social, and religious leader of the community. Beyond the Kimball Block are three more historic blocks all dating before 1873.

After you have explored the historic district, walk down Limerock Street to No. 104 which is the Shore Village Museum. Here you'll find the largest collection of lighthouse and Coast Guard artifacts in the United States. Rockland is a good place for this museum; its own lighthouse has stood in Rockland Harbor since 1888, and the Port of Rockland has long been an active fishing community, earning the title of "Lobster Capital of the World." Every summer a Lobster Festival celebrates the "Harvest of the Sea" with cooking contests, art shows, and a variety of other festivities.

CENTRAL MAINE

Bangor's Historic Districts (31)

Directions: Bangor is located in south central Maine, off I-95. This walk begins in the High Street Historic District at High and Union streets.

Best Season: Spring, summer, fall.

Length: There are five historic districts in Bangor, each 1-mile long and with its own unique atmosphere. Plan on spending at least half a day here.

Degree of Difficulty: Easy.

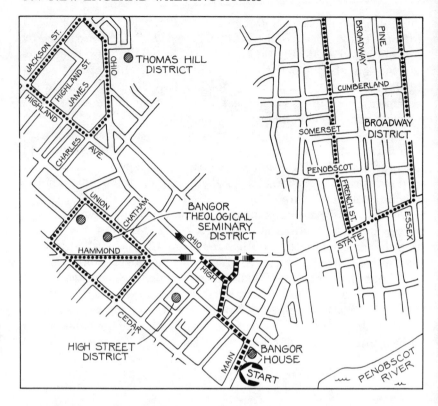

Highlights: Fascinating architecture and elegant old homes recapture Bangor's apex as the "Lumber Capital of the World" in this tour of historic districts.

In 1604 when Samuel de Champlain sailed up the Penobscot ("Place of Rocks") River, he found a peaceful Indian village called Kadesquit on the eastern bank of the Kenduskeag Stream. Champlain observed, made notes, traveled on; 165 years later, the first white settler came. Others followed, and in 1772 the Kenduskeag Plantation was officially born. In 1791, it was given the name *Bangor* by the Reverend Noble, who apparently liked the hymn of the same name. Since then Bangor's history has been one of decided ups and downs.

The first serious "down" occurred in September 1814, when the undefended town was sacked by the British. But the "up" years were to be many as timber became the equivalent of "gold" for residents of Bangor. Before long, lumber from the north was flowing down the Penobscot River at an incredible rate and ending up in Bangor. By 1860, the town was the world's largest lumber port, shipping over 150 million board-feet of lumber a year. Lumber barons basked in the glory of success, creating many of the elegant homes you will see on your walk and making Bangor the cultural center of Maine. By 1880 it had all ended; there was no more timber, the forests were virtually gone.

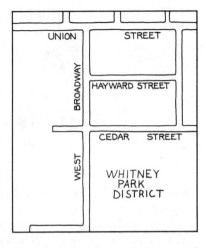

Bangor changed from being a lumber capital to becoming a retail and financial center. Then disaster struck again with the "Great Fire of 1911." The city rebuilt itself and became a wholesale and retail distribution center for eastern Maine and Canada. Today the people of Bangor are enthusiastically restoring the remaining historic buildings and cleaning up the Penobscot River, which had suffered drastically from all the lumber poured into it during the lumber-crazed days. Pollution abatement facilities are being constructed, for example, and the Atlantic salmon have already started to return. In May and June, you can see fishing enthusiasts on State Street at the Bangor Salmon Pool, a natural pool where the salmon come to spawn.

On this walk, nominated by Juliet Kellogg, you will visit five historic districts. The first one, High Street, includes one of the city's oldest houses, the Federal-style Gen. Williams–Rev. Mason House, built in 1825. You'll also see two Greek Revival homes built by Bangor architect Charles G. Bryant, and two homes designed by Richard Upjohn, founder and first president of the American Institute of Architects. One of these, the Thomas A. Hill House, is home to the Bangor Historical Society and is open to the public. The Bangor Theological Seminary District features the second-oldest Congregational Seminary in the United States. In the Whitney Park Historical District, you'll see some of the grand mansions of the lumber barons. This elegant residential district was developed from 1850 to the turn of the century. The Thomas Hill District is the highest point in Bangor and includes one of the city's finest Italianate residences (the Joseph

W. Low House at 51 Highland Street). The Broadway District is special for its elm trees, the last great "nave" of elm trees in Bangor. You'll find a wide variety of architectural styles here, from Federal to Colonial Revival to Beaux Arts.

CENTRAL MAINE

Gulf Hagas (32)

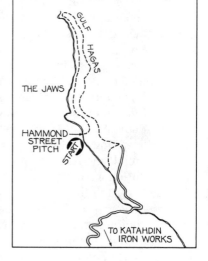

Directions: Located in the heart of Maine in northern Piscataquis County, access to the walk is from Route 11, 5.5 miles north of Brownville Junction. Follow signs to the Katahdin Iron Works (6.75 miles on a gravel road off Route 11). Bear right after passing through the gate at the iron works and continue another 5 or 6 miles to the parking area.

Best Season: Summer and autumn (roads may be impassable in the spring).

Length: 5.2 miles round-trip.

Degree of Difficulty: Moderate.

Highlights: A unique walk in the forest of Maine along a river gorge that has been called the "Grand Canyon of the East."

Owned by the St. Regis and Great Northern Paper Companies, 500 acres of this incredibly beautiful area were set aside for the enjoyment of the public when, in 1969, the deep, narrow slate canyon on the west branch of the Pleasant River was designated as a Registered National Landmark. Sheila Nunley, who nominated this walk, says: "The area *has* to be seen to be fully appreciated. It has often been labeled the 'Grand Canyon of the East' or the 'Little Grand Canyon' and downeasterners are not given to boasting!''

At the beginning of the trail, there is a stand of old-growth white pine now owned by the Nature Conservancy, and along the trail itself you'll pass by several beautiful waterfalls. From the Hammond Street Pitch, you'll stand high above the gorge and look down upon a spectacular view of the canyon. And, at a spot known as The Jaws, you'll see the river narrow as it is forced around a slate spur.

The Katahdin Iron Works are also part of the walk. Here you can see a blast furnace and beehive charcoal burner, now a part of history, but once active in what was a thriving iron works industry.

For a picturesque drive and a visit to some of the most beautiful unspoiled wilderness in all of Maine, head north on Route 11 to the town of Millinocket. From here you can cross a dike to Ambajejus Lake and enter Baxter State Park. The 50-mile Perimeter Road leads through the park, and eventually you will make a loop back to Route 11 at the town of Patten, where the Lumberman Museum, open from mid-October to mid-May, is a wonderful place to get a firsthand look at the lumber industry in Maine.

But the best part of Baxter State Park for walkers is Mount Katahdin (*Ktadn* means "highest land" to the Abnaki Indians). No cars can reach the top: You must get there on foot from Roaring Brook Campground. Don't miss it! Many people consider this mountain to be the most beautiful in the eastern United States (see below).

CENTRAL MAINE

Mt. Katahdin (33)

Directions: Mt. Katahdin is in Baxter State Park, about 80 miles north of Bangor. This walk begins at the Roaring Brook Campground, accessible from the town of Millinocket. From Bangor, take I-95 to Route 11 west. At Millinocket, follow signs to Baxter State Park. The Roaring Brook Campground is on the east side of the park.

Best Season: Mid-August, when "it's not too cold and there aren't too many bugs." (Note that even in August it can be cold and windy at the peak. Bring some warm clothing and a hat.) The park is open

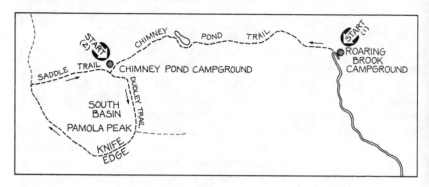

for camping from May 15th to October 15th; from October 15th to December, it is open for day use only. To protect this wilderness area by preventing crowding, reservations are essential at all times of the year. Contact the Reservation Clerk, 64 Balsam Drive, Millinocket, Maine 04462.

Length: Round-trip from Roaring Brook Campground, the walk to the top is about 11 miles.

Degree of Difficulty: Moderately difficult.

Highlights: A great scramble up the rocks to the top of Mt. Katahdin culminates in beautiful views from Maine's highest peak.

Baxter State Park, named for former Governor Percival P. Baxter, who set aside some 200,000 acres for the people of Maine as a wilderness area and wildlife sanctuary, is an area of beautiful, unspoiled wilderness, crowned by Mt. Katahdin, which rises to 5,268 feet and is the highest peak in Maine. You can't drive to the top: The only way to get there is on foot. And it's an experience! Leon Greenman, who is a publisher, writer, editor, and cartographer of history and hiking guides to the New York and New Jersey area, told us about this walk. He is an experienced hiker, having climbed to the top of New Hampshire's Mt. Washington and hiked in the mountains of British Columbia, in Wyoming's Grand Tetons and Wind Rivers, and in the Sangre de Christo Range in New Mexico. His walk to the top of Mt. Katahdin, which he calls "more of a rock scramble than a walk," was, he says, "One of the most fun things I've ever done!"

When Leon and a friend set out to climb to the top of Mt. Katahdin, they did not realize the importance of making a reservation in advance. Fortunately, there had been some last-minute cancellations at the Chimney Pond facility, which is accessible only by foot after a 3.3-mile hike from Roaring Brook. There are lean-tos at Chimney Pond, Leon says, as well as cabin facilities.

From Chimney Pond, Leon suggests you take the Dudley Trail (named for Leroy Dudley, a famous Maine guide of the early 1900s). It's a short (1.3 miles) but wonderful romp over the rocks up to the top. "For anyone who likes to scramble on rocks, it's superb!" Leon exclaims. "There may be easier ways to get to the top, but none is more fun than this one."

Once you reach the ridge, you're on Pamola Peak, named for a vengeful spirit the Indians believed was responsible for the raging winter storms. Any brave who did not return from the top of the mountain was thought to have been a victim of Pamola. The Knife Edge Trail—which Leon says is not really a "knife's edge" at all, rarely narrowing to less than about six feet—runs along the edge of the Great Basin. (Although there may be plenty of room to walk on this trail, the 1,500-foot drops on either side make it no place for anyone suffering from vertigo!) The views here are to the south where the smoke stacks of the lumber mills of Millinocket are plainly visible. "On a clear day it seems as if you can see forever," Leon says. "Ironically," he adds, "when we reached this pristine spot, we found about sixty or seventy people gathered around a politician who was eagerly soliciting votes for one thing or another. Never had anything seemed so incongruous."

When you reach the end of the 1.1-mile Knife Edge Trail, you'll be at the highest peak. Pause for a minute here to reflect that you are standing at the terminus of the legendary Appalachian Trail, which begins 2,000 miles to the south on Georgia's Mount Oglethorpe.

The return to Chimney Pond is via the 2.2-mile Saddle Trail. Check in with the Ranger Station when you get back to let them know you're safe and sound. You can either spend the night at Chimney Pond or hike the 3.3 miles back down to Roaring Brook (depending where you've made your reservations). Watch for moose along this part of the trail. "They're big!" says Leon. "We saw a mother with her calf. They didn't seem afraid of us. It was amazing. I'd never seen a live moose in my life!"

Massachusetts

EASTERN MASSACHUSETTS

Boston by Foot: North End Tour (34)

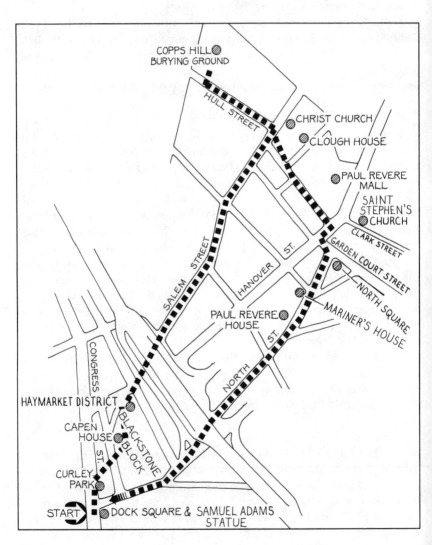

Directions: This walk begins at the statue of Samuel Adams in front of Faneuil Hall on Congress Street in downtown Boston, May 1 to October 31, Saturdays, at 2 p.m., rain or shine, reservations not required. The cost is $5 for adults, $2 for children 6 to 12 years. Other regularly scheduled Boston by Foot tours include: The Heart of the Freedom Trail, Beacon Hill, Copley Square in Back Bay, and Boston by Little Feet. All guides are especially trained volunteers, well-versed in the city's history and architecture. For information on the days, times, and cost, call (617) 367-2345.

Best Season: May through October. If you are in Boston while the Boston by Foot tours are being conducted, don't miss them; you'll get a truly unique perspective of this historic city.

Length: 3 miles round-trip. Allow about an hour and a half for the walk; more if you plan to shop or stop to eat.

Degree of Difficulty: Easy.

Highlights: This walk through Boston's oldest neighborhood imparts the true flavor of Old Boston as you wind through a labyrinth of seventeenth-century streets.

Boston by Foot is a unique nonprofit organization dedicated to sharing Boston's architectural and historical heritage with both those who live in the city and those who come for a visit. Volunteer guides give walkers the "inside story" about the buildings and the people of Boston and about the events that shaped them. Mildred Schmertz, editor of the *Architectural Record,* recently praised the efforts of Boston by Foot, saying, "If beautiful buildings are to live on from generation to generation,...they must be cherished by the broadest segment of the public....The 18th- and 19th-century downtowns of most U.S. cities have vanished with scarcely a trace to be replaced by parking lots, parking garages, office towers and other late 20th-century buildings....Landmark battles are never truly won. Uneconomic buildings and districts are under periodic siege and, unless economic uses can be found, the developers usually win. There is only one force that gives landmarks the relentless, continuous support they must have to survive. That is the force of public will...a public that believes that great works of architecture ultimately be long to them. Boston by Foot does as much as any organization anywhere to help create that public, and it does so with imagination, energy, and a marvelous sense of the fun of it all."

We hope this tribute will inspire people in cities across the country to create their own version of Boston by Foot, for we agree with Ms. Schmertz that in order to preserve the beauty of this country, whether it be in cities or in wilderness areas, we need the support of an educated, concerned, and active public.

Boston's North End Tour, nominated by Polly Flansburgh, begins at the statue of Samuel Adams in front of Faneuil Hall. The statue was sculpted by Boston artist Anne Whitney and is a copy of one she designed for the Capitol in Washington, D.C. From the statue cross Curley Park to the Blackstone Block, a maze of crooked seventeenth-century streets that retains much of the character it had in colonial times when the streets were paved with oyster shells and pebbles. Be sure to note the Union Oyster House at 41 Union Street. Originally known as the Thomas Capen House, the building was constructed around 1714 and was first used as a store for silks and other fabrics. Louis Philippe, later to become King of France, spent part of his exile on the second floor of this house and taught French to wealthy Boston merchants and their daughters. Since 1826, the building has been a restaurant.

At the corner of Salem and Blackstone streets is the Haymarket District, which takes on the character of a festival each weekend as produce and a variety of other products are sold from carts and outdoor stands. This celebration replicates the time when the area served as the site for importing, processing, and distributing meats, fish, and produce.

When you cross over the expressway on the pedestrian tunnel, you will be in the North End, the nation's oldest urban neighborhood, where many of the wealthiest families of the colonial period lived. Walk along Salem Street, and turn left on Hull Street to reach Copps Hill Burying Ground, named for William Copps, who originally owned the land. This is the highest point in the North End and once was the site of a windmill which was used for grinding corn. In 1660, it became a cemetery. Note the bullet holes in some of the tombstones—evidence that the British used them for target practice!

Walk back down Hull Street to Christ Church at the corner of Salem and Hull. Better known as the Old North Church, the building was designed in 1723 and was immortalized by Longfellow in

"Paul Revere's Ride." The interior of the church retains its original beauty, with high box pews and brass chandeliers. Next door is Clough House, designed and built by Ebenezer Clough between 1711 and 1715. Note the outline of the original gambrel roof on the side of the house where the "half house," owned by Benjamin Franklin, once stood.

Continuing down Hull Street, you will come to the Paul Revere Mall, built in 1933 to act as a buffer and reduce the risk of fire to the nearby churches. Bronze plaques on the surrounding walls give a history of the area.

At the corner of Hanover and Clark streets is St. Stephen's Church, designed by Charles Bulfinch in the early 1800s on the site of a small wooden church. St. Stephen's has been home to several religious groups, reflecting the changes in the population of the North End. At first, for ten years, it was a Congregational Church; then it became a Unitarian Church until 1862, when it was bought by the Archdiocese of Boston. As a Roman Catholic church, it has served in turn the Irish, Portuguese, and Italian communities.

From St. Stephen's, walk down Hanover, and turn left onto Garden Court Street to North Square. The Mariner's House at 11 North Square was a hotel for sailors. Opened in 1873, its purpose was to protect sailors from the exorbitant prices charged by some Boston merchants. Next door is Paul Revere House, built around 1680 by John Jeff. Revere bought it in 1770 and owned it for thirty years. The style of the house is Medieval, often called "memory style," because it reflected the memories the colonists had of their homes in England. A walk down North Street will bring you back to Faneuil Hall where the tour began.

EASTERN MASSACHUSETTS

Boston: Black Heritage Trail (35)

Directions: The walk begins at the African Meeting House, 8 Smith Court, Beacon Hill, Boston.

Best Season: Spring, summer, and early fall.

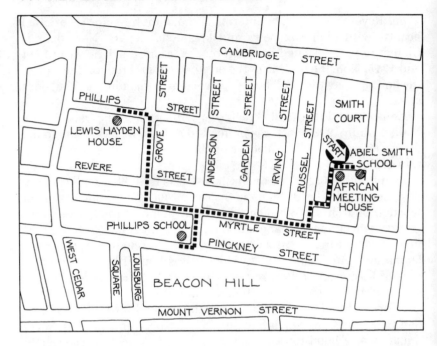

Length: 1.6 miles; but there's so much to see on this walk, you should allow at least half a day.

Degree of Difficulty: Moderate; the terrain is hilly.

Highlights: A personal look at the history of Boston's black community from the American Revolution to the Civil War.

This exceptional trail through Boston's historic black neighborhood gives a perspective on American history unavailable elsewhere. In fact, when Ken Heidelberg nominated the walk, he said: "The Black Heritage Trail deals with information not found in history books. Visitors get a personal touch they don't usually get."

The first blacks to come to Boston were slaves who had been purchased at Providence Isle, a Puritan colony off the coast of Central America. The year was 1638. By 1705, there were some 400 slaves in Boston, as well as a much smaller number of free blacks. By the end of the American Revolution, the numbers had reversed, and there were more free blacks than slaves. In the 1790 census, Massachusetts was the only state in the union to record no slaves.

The African Meeting House, where this walk begins, was completed in 1806 and is the oldest standing black church in America. It served as the heart of Boston's black community for more than fifty years, and from within its walls came an influence that far exceeded its numbers. On January 6, 1832, for example, when the meeting house was also serving as a school, William Lloyd Garrison founded the New England Anti-Slavery Society there, stating: "We have met tonight in this obscure schoolhouse, our members are few and our influence limited; but mark my prediction, Faneuil Hall shall ere long echo with the principles we have set forth. We shall shake the nation by their mighty power."

Other stops along this self-guided walk (an excellent brochure explaining each stop in detail is available at the Afro-American Museum, 46 Joy Street, on the corner of Smith Court) include the Abiel Smith School, which was built in 1834 with money left as a legacy to the city of Boston for the education of black children by Abiel Smith, a white businessman. Another school on the walking tour is the Phillips School at Anderson and Pinckney streets. Built in 1824, this school was closed to black children until 1855, when a bill making segregation in the state's public schools illegal passed the state legislature.

One of the most inspiring stops on the tour is the Lewis and Harriet Hayden House at 66 Phillips Street. Lewis Hayden was born a slave in Lexington, Kentucky, in 1816. He escaped to Detroit on the Underground Railroad and eventually came to Boston. There he lived as a tenant in the house on Phillips Street, which was sold to his wife Harriet in 1865. A Fugitive Slave Law had been passed in 1850 which permitted southern slave owners to retrieve their "property." Outraged by this law, Lewis and Harriet Hayden opened their home to the runaway slaves, and it became a station on the Underground Railroad. The Haydens reportedly kept two kegs of gunpowder in their basement ready to blow up the house if need be, rather than surrender the people they were hiding.

EASTERN MASSACHUSETTS

Old Cambridge Walking Tour (36)

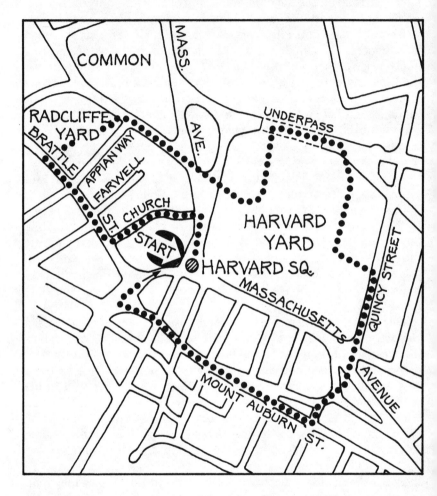

Directions: Cambridge is across the Charles River from Boston. From the Massachusetts Turnpike, exit at Allston/Cambridge, and cross the river to Memorial Drive. Turn left, then right at the second light (J. F. Kennedy Boulevard). Drive straight into Harvard Square to the Cambridge Discovery Information Booth where this walk begins.

Guided tours are given in the mornings and afternoons. For scheduling information, call (617) 497-1630.

Best Season: Summer (the end of June through Labor Day).

Length: About 1 mile; allow about an hour and a half.

Degree of Difficulty: Easy.

Highlights: You'll never forget Old Cambridge after this intimate, historic look at the very heart of Harvard Square.

"Old Cambridge is Harvard Square," explains nominator Charlotte Moore. "It was established in 1630 and has been in flux ever since." You can witness many of the changes that have occurred in Cambridge over more than 350 years by walking its sidewalks and streets, by strolling past the Village Smithy's home and the old churches and structures and by visiting the numerous public art projects that celebrate the town's history. During your walk you may run into some contemporary celebrities who live in Cambridge—writer Robert Parker, for example, of *Spenser* fame, or Julia Child or Tip O'Neill. And if you listen carefully, you may hear the echoes of poets—James Russell Lowell is one who lived in Cambridge, also Henry Wadsworth Longfellow.

Both Lowell and Longfellow were professors at Harvard, and no walk of Cambridge would be complete without a visit to this oldest of American colleges. Harvard was founded in 1636 to train Puritan ministers. It received its name in 1638 in honor of its first benefactor, John Harvard. The college expanded from its original purpose to encompass a more general education during the administration of Charles W. Eliot from 1869 to 1910. During this time, Harvard gained recognition as one of the great universities of the world, a position it still holds today. On this walk, you'll hear some wonderful stories about Harvard—"the flip," for example. You'll also hear more about Cambridge—the underground streams that shape the buildings, the threat of pirates, and the great "ice-cream wars."

The Old Cambridge Walking Tour is given by teenagers who spend eight weeks in training. "They learn about the social and ethnic fabric of the city," Charlotte says, "its historic preservation and economic development issues, its political structure and history. From these guides, you'll learn about the physical development of Cambridge, and you'll follow the footprints of pre-1630 Cambridge in the street patterns of the present-day town. In addition to stories and legends about Harvard, you'll learn about the fight to preserve a 1940 gas station, you'll hear details about the Washington Elm and the witch trials of the 1600s, and you'll discover that there were *two* American Revolutions—one in eating habits, one involving the British!''

EASTERN MASSACHUSETTS

A Walk along the Charles River (37)

Directions: The walk begins on the Charles River campus of Boston University. From the Massachusetts Turnpike, exit at Allston/ Cambridge, and follow signs to Cambridge. Turn right at the first set of lights (Soldiers Field Road/ Storrow Drive), and follow Storrow Drive to the Kenmore exit. Turn right at the first set of traffic

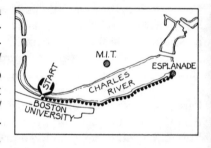

lights onto Beacon Street, and take the left fork into Kenmore Square. Bear right onto Commonwealth Avenue and park near the Boston University Information Center at 771 Commonwealth Avenue. Public transportation is also available via any Green Line subway station in downtown Boston. Take the B train, heading toward Kenmore Square, and exit at the second or third stop after Kenmore.

Best Season: Spring.

Length: 3 to 4 miles round-trip. Allow at least an hour.

Degree of Difficulty: Easy.

Highlights: This walk along the Charles River is scenic, educational, ever-changing, and lots of fun.

"Where can one boast of having it all?" nominator Flora Pignatiello asks rhetorically, for she knows the answer: "Right here along the Charles River!" Flora is the leader of a walking group called Champions on Foot, whose members meet every Tuesday, rain or shine, for a walk. "We feel that a walk can be rewarding, physically, mentally, and morally," Flora explains. "And we have become a family, sharing many of the same interests. Our weekly walks have brought back the sense of humor some of us had lost due to the loneliness that is very often the major pain of being an elder. The walks have somehow brought out our 'hidden talents.'"

Flora and her group have discovered one of the elements in the "magic" of walking—companionship and sharing. One of the walks they most like to share together is the one that follows a wide path along the Charles River. There's so much to see, and it's always a little different. "Up and down the Charles River something is always going on," Flora says. "There are university crew races and regattas—all sorts of boats—and as you walk along the shore you are greeted by various species of ducks and birds."

The walk starts at Boston University, which began as a theological seminary in 1839. Today some 37,000 students attend the school, making it the fifth-largest independent university in the United States. Before or after your walk along the river, you may want to spend some time visiting this historic campus which includes the largest bookstore in New England, a turn-of-the-century-style tree-lined promenade, a Tudor castle, and an art gallery featuring some of the finest exhibits of contemporary art to be found in Boston. In the plaza of the Marsh Chapel stands a tribute to one of the university's most outstanding alumni, Dr. Martin Luther King. "It's a striking piece of workmanship," Flora says. "A bronze structure consisting of flying doves to signify peace." During the academic year, tours of the campus are offered from the Visitors' Reception Center, 121 Bay State Road, Monday through Friday, every hour on the hour from 10 a.m. to 3 p.m., and on Saturday at 10 and 11 a.m. and at noon. In the summer, the tours are held Monday through Friday from 11 a.m. to 3 p.m.

From Boston University, follow the path along the river eastward. Across the river you will be able to see another distinguished university—the Massachusetts Institute of Technology (MIT). Founded in 1861, MIT has always enjoyed a reputation as one of the finest schools in the country, and its influence in the fields of science and engineering is renowned. Student-guided tours of the campus are given Monday through Friday at 10 a.m. and 2 p.m.

Enjoy your walk along the river at whatever pace you choose—a leisurely stroll, a brisk walk, a race walk, or an aerobic workout. But be sure to take time out to observe the activity on the river. The walk ends at the Esplanade, where you'll find a memorial to orchestra conductor Arthur Fiedler, who first began concerts in the Esplanade bandshell in 1929. The next year, 1930, Fiedler became director of the Boston Pops Orchestra, a position he held until his death nearly fifty years later. The memorial portrait of Fiedler is made of layers of aluminum, and Flora says it is very impressive. "When the sun shines on it, it's as if Mr. Fiedler were right here, talking to his musicians."

EASTERN MASSACHUSETTS

A Presidential Walk in Brookline (38)

Directions: A suburb of Boston, Brookline can be reached from the Allston-Brighton exit of I-90 (Massachusetts Turnpike). Turn left on Harvard Street, and continue to Beals Street. The walk begins at the J.F.K. National Historic Site, 83 Beals Street.

Best Season: Spring through fall.

Length: About 1 mile one way. Allow one-half to three-quarters of an hour.

Degree of Difficulty: Easy.

Highlights: Beautiful Victorian homes and gardens blend with historic sites in this walk through Brookline.

This walk, nominated by Charlotte Millman and Jean Kramer, begins at the birthplace and childhood home of John Fitzgerald Kennedy, the thirty-fifth president of the United States. The home, a National Historic Site maintained by the National Park Service, is open to the public every day (except Thanksgiving, Christmas, and

New Year's Day) from 10 a.m. to 4:30 p.m. Admission is $1 for adults; children under 16 and seniors are admitted free.

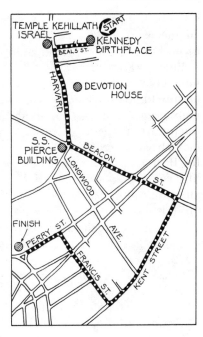

From the Kennedy Home, walk left one block to Harvard Street. At the corner of Beals and Harvard streets is Temple Kehillath Israel, the first synagogue built in Brookline. Turn left (south) on Harvard Street, a busy commercial thoroughfare, and stop at No. 347, the Edward Devotion House. Built in the eighteenth century, the Devotion House is managed by the Brookline Historical Society and is open to the public on Tuesdays and Thursdays from 2 to 5 p.m. Behind the Devotion House is the Edward Devotion School, a public school attended by both President Kennedy and his older brother, Joseph.

Cross Harvard Street and continue south to No. 314–320, the Arcade Building. Constructed in 1926, the building features a skylight atrium surrounded by shops and offices. The interior represents an almost-unaltered picture of small shop design of the 1920s. On the northwest corner of Beacon and Harvard Streets, known as Coolidge Corner, is the S.S. Pierce Building, which was constructed during the year 1898–1899 and has recently been restored. A town landmark, this building, with its impressive clock tower, once housed a venerable food emporium, the S.S. Pierce Store. In its heyday, it was known for exotic imported delicacies which could be ordered from anywhere in the world and delivered to your home.

Cross Beacon Street and peek inside the Bay Bank Norfolk Trust Company Building, a fine example of the Art Deco style, then continue east on Beacon to Kent Street, and turn right. (Temple Ohabei Shalom, the home of Boston's oldest Hebrew congregation, is on the corner of Beacon and Kent.) Walk south on Kent Street, past Longwood Square, where you'll see a stand of beech trees planted by David Sears in the mid-nineteenth century. There are many examples of splendid Victorian houses in this area, most of which have recently been converted to condominiums.

Facing east at the corner of Longwood and Kent, you can see the Longwood Towers apartment complex, which was built in the 1920s, and was known for many years as the home of the "newly-wed and nearly dead" (young couples and the elderly). In the distance, across the Muddy River, you can see some of Boston's most famous hospitals. Continue south on Kent Street to Francis Street, and turn right (west). Pass the Lawrence School, and stop to rest at the newly renovated Longwood Playground, where you'll find benches under the shade of tall trees.

From Longwood Playground, walk down Francis Street to Perry Street, and turn left to number No. 85. This is the home of Michael Dukakis, governor of Massachusetts and presidential candidate in 1988.

This ends the tour; if you would like to know about other walking tours of Brookline, nominators Charlotte Millman and Jean Kramer invite you to stop in at the Brookline Council on Aging, 61 Park Street, or call (617) 730-2111.

EASTERN MASSACHUSETTS

Breakheart Reservation (39)

Directions: Breakheart Reservation is located in the town of Saugus, which is on Route 1, just north of Boston. Take the Lynn-Fells Parkway off Route 1, and turn right on Forest Street. Park Headquarters are at 177 Forest Street.

Best Season: Year-round, weather permitting.

Length: The time you spend at Breakheart Reservation will vary. There are miles of trail within the reservation, including pathways around two lakes, loop trails through the forest, and a river trail along the Saugus River.

Degree of Difficulty: Easy to moderately difficult.

Highlights: An exciting program of nature walks and pristine natural beauty make Breakheart Reservation a wonderful getaway place from the nearby populated areas.

Breakheart is one of ten reservations around Greater Boston that is maintained by the Metroparks Division of the Metropolitan District Commission. Metroparks, which originated with a proposal from landscape architect Charles Eliot in 1892, is a unique organization which preserves and maintains a total of 14,700 acres around Greater Boston, as well as part of the Boston Harbor Islands State Park and other sites, including parkways, rivers, beaches, and playgrounds. As a result, the people of Greater Boston and those who come for a visit can enjoy the peacefulness of nature just minutes from crowded urban areas.

Breakheart Reservation is one of the newest in the Metroparks system, and it is a favorite of nominators Vico Milano and Flora Bishop, who often participate in the many nature programs and guided walks the reservation offers. Each of the programs is geared to a particular season. In late winter, for example, you can take a "maple-sugarin'" tour, during which you'll learn to tap maple trees and discover how to turn sap into syrup. There are spring hikes around Pearce Lake and Silver Lake, and a summer bird walk along the Saugus River.

Sometimes a walk will take you back in time, and you'll hear tales about the history of the area. There's a story about a murder which took place in 1900, for example, and tales of Ben Johnson's hunting lodges. You'll learn about the history of the reservation as well. The rocky hills around Breakheart were formed millions of years ago, but vegetation and animal life did not appear until the last glaciers melted some 10,000 years ago. The name *Breakheart* was given to the area by Civil War soldiers who were training here and found the place "lonely and remote from civilization." Most hikes begin at 2 p.m. and leave from Park Headquarters. The walks last from 1 to 2 hours. For more information, call (617) 233-0834.

Today Breakheart Reservation is right in the heart of civilization, yet it still provides a "lonely and remote" place for city-weary visitors who seek the solitude of nature.

EASTERN MASSACHUSETTS

Blue Hills Reservation: Houghton's Pond (40)

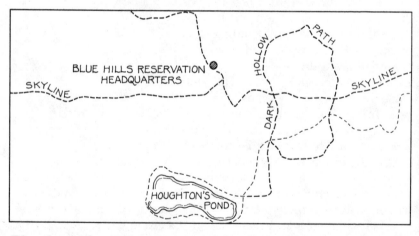

Directions: Blue Hills Reservation is less than 9 miles from the center of Boston. The Houghton's Pond Section, where this walk takes place, is accessible via Route 128. Take exit 3, and follow Blue Hill River Road to the parking area.

Best Season: Spring and fall.

Length: Less than 1½ miles. Allow about an hour for the walk around the pond, but you'll probably want to spend all day in this lovely place.

Degree of Difficulty: Easy.

Highlights: This is a wonderful place for an all-day outing with family or friends. Picnicking, swimming, and boating are all available, and there's a nice pathway to follow for a walk around the pond.

Blue Hills Reservation encompasses 5,800 acres and is the largest public open space within 35 miles of Boston. Administered by the Metropolitan District Commission's Park Division, Blue Hills is divided into seven sections. The most popular area is probably that of Great Blue Hill, which rises 635.5 feet above sea level and is the highest point along the Atlantic Coast from southern Maine to Florida. Known affectionately as "Big Blue," hikers climb to its summit almost every day of the year. Not only does Great Blue Hill give its name to the reservation, it is also responsible for the name of the state: *Massachusetts* comes from an Algonquin Indian word meaning "among the great hills," a reference to the Blue Hills.

To get a walking overview of the reservation, take the 9-mile Sky Line Foot Path which traverses the entire Blue Hill range from east to west and crosses many of the summits, including that of Big Blue. But for a wonderful day's outing with family or friends, nominator Charlotte Graham prefers Houghton's Pond, where in addition to a pleasant walk around the pond you can swim from a supervised public beach (the only supervised fresh water swimming within the Blue Hills) and enjoy the historic Refreshment Pavilion. There are picnic areas (with fireplaces), three playgrounds around the pond, tennis courts, and a softball field. The pond is stocked with trout, and during the summer those who like to fish will also find bass, perch, and sunfish.

The walking path around the pond links up with longer trails, such as the Great Dome Trail and Dark Hollow Path, so it is possible to hike for miles and explore a wide variety of terrain and habitat. An excellent trail map is available at the Trailside Museum or at Park Headquarters. It gives the length of the various trails, the hiking time, and tells you what to expect along the route. It also asks you to "take only memories and leave only footprints." If you do plan to walk on any of the longer trails, don't go alone, wear good shoes, and carry ample water. "And bring your binoculars," Charlotte suggests. "You'll want them for bird watching."

EASTERN MASSACHUSETTS

Wellesley College: Alexandra Botanic
Garden and Hunnewell Arboretum (41)

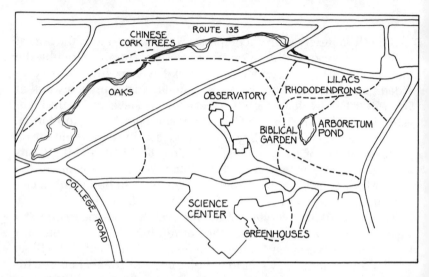

Directions: The gardens and arboretum are located just off Route 135 in Wellesley. From Boston, take Route 9 to 135.

Best Season: Spring through fall.

Length: 2 miles. Allow about two hours.

Degree of Difficulty: Easy.

Highlights: This is a wonderful walk through a variety of different kinds of gardens and greenhouses which contain the finest collection of tropical plants in New England.

This delightful walk was nominated by June Gehrig who says, "It's an absolutely perfect walk for seniors because it's easy (there are no hills), and the combination of gardens and greenhouses along with the enjoyable walk make it wonderful for everyone of all ages."

The Margaret C. Ferguson Greenhouses include fifteen glass houses with over 1,000 different kinds of plants. Each greenhouse has its own separate temperature control so that different climates can be created. You'll see plants from the arid desert as well as those from the subtropics, and just about everything in between, including magnificent orchids and lush green ferns. The greenhouses were built in 1922 and renovated in 1983 to provide modern energy-efficient greenhouse construction.

In the botanical gardens, you'll find over 500 species of woody plants and a collection of specimen trees and shrubs which includes American white and English oaks, lindens, tulip trees, bald cypresses, and Chinese golden larches. In the spring, azaleas, lilacs, viburnums, hollies, weeping cherries, and rhododendrons display a dazzling array of color throughout the gardens. Near the Arboretum Pond is a fascinating Biblical Garden with an exhibit of many of the plants mentioned in the Bible.

The many acres of native trees and wildflowers serve as a natural laboratory for the study of ecology, botany, and zoology, and several of the greenhouses are reserved for class study and research by faculty and students of Wellesley College. Interestingly, the college, which was chartered in 1870, was the first women's college in the country to have scientific laboratories.

The Alexandra Botanic Garden and Hunnewell Arboretum are open every day of the year from 8:30 a.m. to 4:30 p.m. For more information, call (617) 235-0320 (ext. 3094).

EASTERN MASSACHUSETTS
Black Pond Preserve (42)

Directions: The preserve is located in Norwell, southeast of Boston. Take Route 3 south, and follow signs to Route 123 west, which leads to Norwell Center and becomes Norwell's Main Street. Continue west on Main Street to Lincoln Street. Turn right at Mount Blue Street, and continue to the Black Pond Preserve entrance sign on your left. A parking area is located across the street from the entrance.

Best Season: Spring, summer, and fall.

Length: 2 to 3 miles. Allow about an hour.

Degree of Difficulty: Easy; there's a good path and a boardwalk.

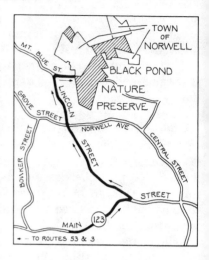

Highlights: An unusual sphagnum moss bog covers part of Black Pond with a floating spongelike mat filled with orchids, pitcher plants, sundew, and other oddities of the bog environment.

Black Pond, which is actually a glacial kettlehole with extremely acid water, affords a unique opportunity to learn about bogs, which for many of us are places that swallow you up in horror movies or science fiction books. And they are usually pretty far away—like in England or on another planet. This bog is in Massachusetts!

Black Pond Preserve includes an old meadow, some swamps, and a woodland forest, but nominator Trish Livingston finds the shaking sphagnum bog the most compelling. "Pitcher plants, sundews, and bladderworts eat insects before my very eyes," she says. "In May, rhodora, cassandra, and arethusa show their white or pink flowers." Trish cautions you to be sure to remain on the boardwalk as you observe the bog; it is a highly fragile area and must not be disturbed.

As these bog plants grow, die, decay, and sink to the bottom of Black Pond, the water is gradually replaced with peat; in another few hundred years, there will be no open water remaining at the pond.

Black Pond Preserve was the first nature conservancy preserve in Massachusetts. Further information about the preserve, as well as a *Discovery and Information Guide,* may be obtained by writing the Audubon Society, 2000 Main Street, Marshfield, MA 02050, or by calling them at (617) 837-9400.

EASTERN MASSACHUSETTS

Hingham Walking Tour (43)

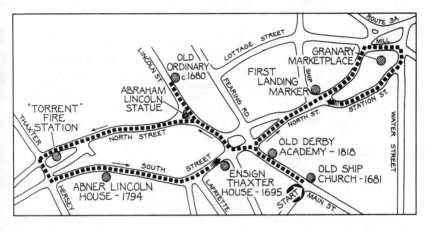

Directions: From Boston, take Route 3 south to exit 14 or 15, and follow signs to Hingham Center and Route 228, which becomes Main Street. The walk begins at the Old Ship Church on Main Street.

Best Season: Spring through fall.

Length: The distance is short, but allow several hours to visit the historic town of Hingham.

Degree of Difficulty: Easy.

Highlights: History and beautiful scenery blend perfectly in this charming walk.

When the first settlers arrived at Hingham in the 1600s, they called it Bare Cove because of the mud flats produced at low tide. Shortly thereafter, perhaps in a mood of loneliness or homesickness, they renamed it Hingham after their homeland in Norfolk, England. In the early days of Hingham's history, the town was a thriving maritime center, its wharves lined with warehouses, ship chandleries, barrel cooperages, salt works, and fish packing operations. Today, as you will see from the pleasure boats, swimmers, and fishing enthusiasts, Hingham has become a place primarily to have fun.

This walk, nominated by Brooks Kelly, begins at the Old Ship Church on Main Street. Built in 1681, it is the oldest wooden church still in use in America. The cemetery in back contains the graves of Hingham's earliest families.

Continue up Main Street to the Hingham Historical Society, located in a building which dates from 1816 and which was once Old Derby Academy, the country's first coeducational school. The heart of Hingham's historical district is a little farther on where Main Street meets North, South, and Lincoln streets. Begin your exploration of this area at Lincoln Street, where the statue of Abraham Lincoln commemorates the fact that President Lincoln's ancestor, Samuel Lincoln, was a Hingham settler.

A short distance to the right, at 21 Lincoln Street, is the Old Ordinary, which was built around 1680 and was used for many years as an "ordinary" or tavern. Today it is a museum filled with antiques and boasting a formal garden, designed by Frederick Law Olmsted, Jr., outside. From here, retrace your steps back down Lincoln Street to North Street, where you'll find a wide variety of architectural homes, including the Gen. Benjamin Lincoln House, which was built in 1667, and Odd Fellows Hall where, in 1868, the ordination of the first woman minister in New England took place. Return to Main Street via South Street.

Before leaving Hingham, be sure to visit the Granary Marketplace at North, Mill, Water, and Station streets. Here under one roof is a picturesque shopping arcade with numerous specialty shops.

SOUTHEASTERN MASSACHUSETTS

Plymouth Walking Tour (44)

Directions: From Boston, take Route 3 south to the Plymouth exit. The walk begins at Plymouth Rock.

Best Season: Spring through fall (summers can be crowded, however).

Length: About 3 miles. Allow a full day to really experience the history of the place.

Degree of Difficulty: Easy.

Highlights: History blended with beautiful scenery and contemporary endeavors make Plymouth an unusual place.

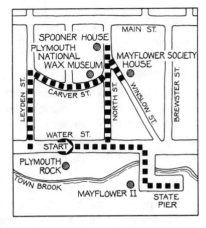

This walk begins, appropriately enough, at Plymouth Rock, where on December 21, 1620, the first Pilgrims stepped ashore and began what we call today "American history." The statue near the rock is of William Bradford, historian and long-time governor of Plymouth Colony.

From the Rock, walk north to State Pier and board *Mayflower II*, a full-scale replica of the type of ship the Pilgrims sailed. On board you'll find men and women who dress, speak, and think like the crew and passengers of the *Mayflower*. It's an incredible experience to talk with them and to realize just how different our customs and way of life have become, for these guides are brilliant in their characterizations of seventeenth-century folk, rarely—if ever—slipping into the wrong time period, despite daily efforts by visitors to trick them.

Cross Water Street and walk up North Street to Winslow Street and the Mayflower Society House, which was built in 1754 by Edward Winslow, the great-grandson of a *Mayflower* passenger. Nominator Brooks Kelly tells us that: "A tour of the nine-room home is like visiting two houses: The front is authentic 1754 Colonial, and the rear is 1898 Victorian. Ralph Waldo Emerson was married in this house, and Dr. Charles Jackson, Emerson's brother-in-law, a resident of the house at one time, "discovered" ether. (Controversy surrounds the discoverer of ether, with three men claiming the title—one of them was Dr. Jackson.)

Across North Street is the Spooner House, which was built in 1749 and was occupied by Spooners until James Spooner died in 1954 and left the house to the Plymouth Antiquarian Society. For more than 200 years, the same family lived in the same house; that may be an American record.

Walk back a short distance now, and follow Carver Street to Cole's Hill, the original burial ground for the settlers. During their first hard winter, the Pilgrims buried their dead in unmarked graves so the Indians would not know how depleted their ranks had become. Atop the hill is a statue of Massasoit, chief of the Wampanoags, who befriended the Pilgrims and assured their survival that first winter. Also on the hill is the Plymouth National Wax Museum with more than twenty-five life-size scenes of Pilgrim history. Thirty-seven steps lead down the hill and back to Plymouth Rock.

This walk covers just a few of the many highlights of Plymouth and the surrounding area. Wander off on your own and explore; imagine yourself a Pilgrim or a Wampanoag. Plymouth is a place of "living history." For more information, write Plymouth County Development Council, P.O. Box 1620, Pembroke, MA 02359.

SOUTHEASTERN MASSACHUSETTS

Cape Cod: Provincetown Dunes Walk (45)

Directions: On Cape Cod, take Route 6 to Provincetown. The walk begins on Commercial Street.

Best Season: Summer and fall.

Length: From 10 to 18 miles. Allow between four and six hours.

Degree of Difficulty: Moderate to moderately difficult.

Highlights: An exhilarating and breathtakingly beautiful walk with spectacular views of the ocean and the entire tip of Cape Cod.

The enormous popularity of Cape Cod has somewhat dimmed its appeal for those who seek a quiet spot. However, the beauty of the place, combined with today's deeper concern for preserving our nat-

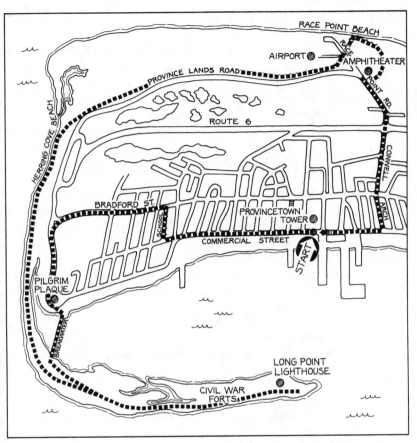

ural heritage makes this area very much worth a visit. Chances are, just like Amiel Singer, who sent us his own personal walking tour, you'll return year after year. Be careful, though, to stay on the path and off the dunes. The dunes are very fragile, and even a bare foot may disturb their well-being.

Amiel's walk begins on Commercial Street in historic Province-town, an artists' colony filled with charming shops and good restaurants. After you've had your fill of browsing and/or eating, find your way to School Street, turn right and walk to Bradford Street. Continue along Bradford to Route 6A, pausing to take in the many examples of Colonial architecture along the way.

When you come to the Moors, walk left to the Provincetown Circle at the Provincetown Inn. Here you'll find the beginning of a mile-long breakwater that leads to the first of three Provincetown lighthouses. The dike is made up of big boulders, so watch your step. From the lighthouse, there are splendid views of the bay and of Provincetown, amid the calls of birds soaring all around or searching for food in the sand.

Now, walk right along the beach with the ocean on one side of you and the dunes on the other. At Herring Cove Beach, about 3 or 4 miles farther on, there is a rest station. From here you can return to Provincetown via Route 6A to Bradford Street or walk on, following the bike path through the dunes. Amiel, of course, suggests you go on. Your walk through the dunes will take you over many hills, through shaded areas, even a few tunnels, and past the Provincetown airport, where you can take a small plane up for an aerial view of the Cape.

From the airport, the path leads up a hill to Race Point Beach where from high cliffs, you have the best view of all of the ocean and the entire tip of Cape Cod. A path leads down to the beach and along another bike path, past beautiful ponds and out to Route 6. From here it's an easy walk back to the Provincetown Tower in the heart of Provincetown.

Amiel "discovered" this walk four years ago when he was staying in Provincetown for the first time with friends who went off one day on a biking excursion. ("At the time," Amiel says, "I didn't own a bike.") Left to his own devices, Amiel decided to take a walk. "I kept a log of where I went and what I saw and did along the way. I just kept on walking without realizing the distance I covered, aware only of the spectacular natural environment I was encountering along the route. Since that summer, I have always made time every year to return to Provincetown and take this walk."

SOUTHEASTERN MASSACHUSETTS

Cape Cod Canal (46)

Directions: There are several access points to this walk. To walk the full distance from Buzzards Bay to Scusset Beach, start at Buzzards Bay off Route 6 in Wareham. Route 6 can be picked up from Route 3 out of Boston, Route 195 out of Providence, Rhode Island, and Route 495 out of central Massachusetts.

Best Season: Year-round, weather permitting.

Length: 7.7 miles one way.

Degree of Difficulty: Easy; there is a well-paved walkway, rest areas along the way, and only some small hills. All ages and the handicapped can enjoy this walk.

Highlights: The Cape Cod Canal walk encompasses scenic beauty, local color, sites of historic interest, and lots of nice people.

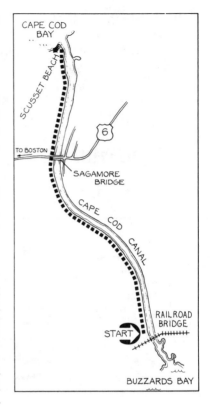

Louise Paolella of the Middleboro Council on Aging's Walking Club nominated this scenic walk along Cape Cod Canal. It follows an eight-foot-wide service road which is operated by the U.S. Army Corps of Engineers. Open only to foot traffic the Canal road is a favorite with many local walking clubs. "This walk is especially nice," Louise says, "because along the route you can always stop to rest and enjoy the scenery. You're sure to meet people fishing or biking, both local people and tourists. You can also break away from the path to do some shopping at the many specialty shops in the towns along the way."

From Buzzards Bay, where the walk begins, you can see the Cape Cod Railtrain, which crosses the canal via an elevator bridge. Other sights you are likely to see as you follow the road along the canal include large tankers, fishing vessels, and cruise ships. In the spring, the wildflowers bring lots of brilliant color to the walk, and year-round you will be able to spot a variety of birds and animals. Quaint little Cape Cod cottages are visible from the path, and at one point there's a wooden walkway which extends over the canal and is used for fishing. Rest rooms and parking areas are available at several access locations.

If you take this walk at any time from mid-May through September, you may want to go on one of the ranger-led bike hikes that are offered. They begin at 10 a.m. at the North Service Road access point adjacent to the Buzzards Bay Town Park on the northeast side of the Railroad Bridge.

SOUTHEASTERN MASSACHUSETTS

Cape Cod Rail Trail (47)

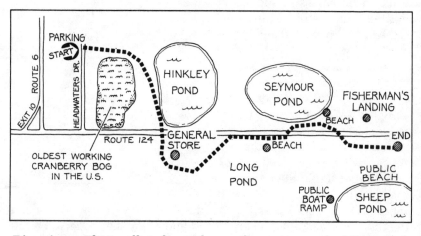

Directions: This walk is located near the eastern end of Cape Cod, just before the sandy peninsula hooks north. Take exit 10 from Route 6 on Cape Cod, and turn left on Route 124. Take another left on Headwaters Drive, and park in the bike trail parking lot on your left.

Best Season: Fall. The foliage is beautiful and you can watch the cranberry harvesting.

Length: 4 miles round-trip. Allow about two hours.

Degree of Difficulty: Easy; the walking surface is a wide, blacktop hiking trail. Bring a jacket or sweatshirt with a hood because the weather and walking conditions change quickly during the walk, from sheltered woods, to windy open areas, to sunny and warm pond beaches.

Highlights: This walk offers a spectacular variety of natural beauty.

This trail, which begins adjacent to the oldest working cranberry bog in the United States, follows an old right-of-way of the Cape Cod Railroad. All along the route, you'll be in a lovely country setting with almost continuous water views. The first pond you see is Hinkley Pond on your left. After crossing Route 124, you may choose to stop at the General Store, which was originally the railroad station. (Be careful crossing Route 124: the trail comes out of the woods, and Route 124 curves at the store.) Today the General Store caters to walkers and bikers, providing picnic tables outside and various supplies and food. You're likely to meet people from all over the world at this delightful social spot.

From the General Store, the trail rises above Route 124 at Long Pond. Recross 124 at the beach, and walk along the edge of Seymour Pond before crossing 124 again. Walk right, off the trail, onto Fisherman's Landing Road, and head downhill to Sheep Pond, where you may want to relax for a while on the sandy beach before retracing your steps back the way you came.

Sybil lives in nearby Harwich and often takes this walk with other members of a walking group whose members enjoy a chance to explore the outdoors. The Cape Cod Rail Trail is a favorite with everyone. "It offers the contradiction of crossing areas that seem remote and wild but are adjacent to a local, heavily trafficked road," she says. "The views are ever-changing panoramas of sky, water, bog, and ponds. Colors change continuously, and are especially brilliant in crisp fall weather. The light changes, too, as you emerge from shaded woods into the bright sunlight. And even our noisy walking group doesn't drive the birds and ducks away. This is the most concentrated, physically beautiful area to walk on Cape Cod."

WESTERN MASSACHUSETTS

The Mount: Edith Wharton's Home in the Berkshires (48)

Directions: The Mount is located on Plunkett Street in Lenox, at the junction of Routes 7 and 7A. From the main gate, follow signs to the parking area.

Best Season: Summer and fall.

Length: About ⅓ mile. Allow approximately three-quarters of an hour, more if you want to explore the woods.

Degree of Difficulty: Easy.

Highlights: This walk through the private world of Pulitzer Prize–winning novelist Edith Wharton takes you back to turn-of-the-century elegance.

"Edith Wharton was very much drawn to the beautiful Berkshire countryside," explains nominator Scott Marshall, a Wharton scholar and assistant director of the Edith Wharton Restoration. "She used it as a setting for some her most famous novels, including *Ethan Frome* (1911) and *Summer* (1917)." The peacefulness and quiet beauty of the area inspired Wharton to greater heights of creativity, and as

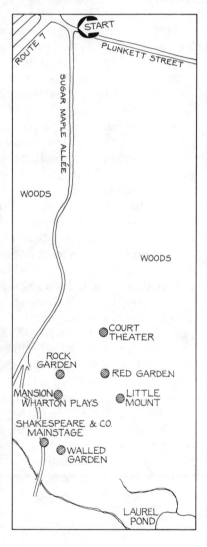

you walk in and around her home, called The Mount, you, too, may become inspired.

Wharton began developing the estate in 1901 with her niece, landscape gardener Beatrix Farrand, who later designed the magnificent gardens at Dumbarton Oaks in Washington, D.C. Farrand created the drive and approach to The Mount in three parts: From the white gates there is an 800-foot-long allée of sugar maples, then a twisting picturesque drive through a heavily wooded area of vinca and periwinkle, to a clearing and a final sweeping approach, along clipped green lawns, to the mansion.

Below the house, and designed to complement it, are two formal gardens, the major flower garden called the Red Garden and a *giardino segreto*, an Italian walled "secret" garden. A meadow below the gardens stretches to Laurel Pond. "The gardens are currently under restoration," Scott says, "but their original outline and their own 'garden magic' as Edith Wharton described it, may still be sensed. A passionate gardener throughout her lifetime, Wharton not only created gardens but also wrote about them in perceptive and scholarly fashion. Her 1904 *Italian Villas and Their Gardens*, with lovely illustrations by artist Maxfield Parrish, is still one of the touchstones of garden literature."

In addition to visiting the house itself, which frequent visitor Henry James described as "a delicate French chateau mirrored in a Massachusetts pond," you can walk in the woods that make up an extensive part of the 50-acre property. Scott tells us that "Edith Wharton loved the landscape and used its metaphors frequently in her fiction. As she explained in her autobiography: 'Life in the country is the only state which has always completely satisfied me....Now I was to know the joys of six or seven months a year among fields and woods of my own...(and) the deep joy of communion with the earth....The Mount was to give me country cares and joys, long happy rides and drives through the wooded lanes of that loveliest region, the companionship of a few dear friends, and the freedom from trivial obligations which was necessary if I was to go on with my writing.'" The paths throughout the woods are used by walkers year-round, by horseback riders in the summer, and by cross-country skiers in the winter. During the summer a theatrical troupe, Shakespeare & Company, performs on the grounds, and plays based on Wharton's life and work are given in the drawing room and on the terrace.

You will love this chance to experience the private world of Edith

Wharton, the first woman novelist to receive a Pulitzer Prize (for *The Age of Innocence*, 1920). "It is a special world of manicured lawns and gardens combined into the rolling Berkshire countryside, and of woods and meadows dotted by small streams and shining ponds," Scott says. "It was—and still is—a place of creative energy, of great beauty, and of inspiration."

WESTERN MASSACHUSETTS

Bartholomew's Cobble: Ledges Trail (49)

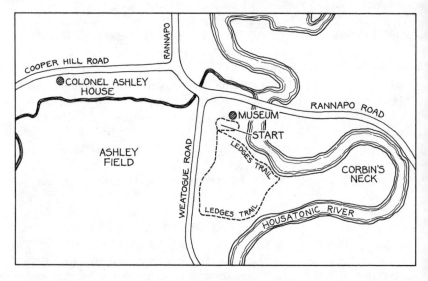

Directions: From Sheffield Center, take Route 7 south for 1.1 miles. Turn right on Route 7A, and follow signs to Bartholomew's Cobble on Weatogue Road. The entrance and parking area are on the left.

Best Season: The Cobble is open from mid-April to mid-October.

Length: ½ mile. It can be walked in about three-quarters of an hour, but there are shortcuts or "long cuts," depending on your mood—so allow several hours.

Degree of Difficulty: From easy to difficult; trails go from dramatic outcroppings to meadows of wildflowers.

Highlights: Scenic 100-foot-high hills of marble and quartzite about 500 million years old offer fabulous views of the Housatonic River on this beautiful walk in the Berkshires.

There are twenty stations along this diverse interpretive trail which passes through a grove of hemlocks, skirts along giant cliffs, and splits off from the Housatonic at a dramatic oxbow bend. From there a verdant meadow is visible, and farther on there are caves. You'll see a variety of woodland plants, including trillium, mayapple, hepaticus, harebells, milkweed, and dogwood. Remember, just look, don't pick anything. Nesting places for birds and ferns can be seen in the rock cavities, and the "ferocious" ant lions await their prey in the sand craters. Continuing along the trail, you'll come upon a 100-plus-year-old cedar tree.

"Though I have been to Bartholomew's Cobble a number of times," says Cecily Mills, who nominated this walk, "each time has brought new experiences. Being a nature lover, I have become intrigued with the discovery and identification of plants, wildflowers, trees, shrubs, and vines. The late C. A. Weatherby, curator of Harvard's Gray Herbarium, catalogued over 800 species of plants; I'm not even halfway there yet. Probably the largest concentration of ferns can be found at the Cobble, but I'm only beginning to understand the differences between the fifty-three varieties. I used to think that goldenrod was just goldenrod. In my own field at home, I've identified eight different varieties; there are sixteen varieties to be found on the Ledges Trail."

There are 277 acres in Bartholomew's Cobble, so Cecily plans her visits there with a purpose. "Picnics are always a favorite," she says, "often with visiting guests. Before we start on a trail, we visit the Bailey's Natural History Museum for an overview. And, if we're there at the right time (Wednesday through Sunday), we find the warden-naturalist who answers all our endless questions."

For the first-time visitor, it's always a surprise to meet an unafraid, friendly chickadee. "They fearlessly alight on your outstretched palm," Cecily says. "You can examine every feather as they watch you with their bright black eyes."

Before leaving the Cobble, visit the Colonel John Ashley House on Cooper Hill Road. Built in 1735, it is the oldest dwelling in

Berkshire County. Beautifully restored with Colonial furnishings and a pottery collection, the house contains its original wood paneling.

"Thousands of visitors come to explore this exceptional natural wildlife area each year," Cecily concludes. "I feel so privileged to have it within my reach." For further information about the Cobble, write the Berkshire Visitors' Bureau, Berkshire Common, Pittsfield, MA 01201, or call (413) 443-9186.

WESTERN MASSACHUSETTS

Mt. Holyoke and Mt. Norwottuck (50)

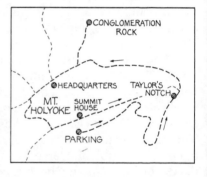

Directions: Mt. Holyoke is located in the Joseph Allen Skinner State Park, part of the larger Holyoke Range State Park. From I-91, take exit 19, and head east on Route 9 to Hadley. Pick up Route 47 south, and watch for signs to the park, which is about 5 miles from the intersection of Route 9 at Hadley Center. Mt. Norwottuck, farther east along the Holyoke Range can be reached by traveling a few miles east from Hadley along Route 9 to Amherst. In Amherst, pick up Route 116 going south, and watch for signs to the Notch Visitors Center, which is on your left about 4 or 5 miles from Amherst as you cross the crest of the Holyoke Range. At the center, trail maps are available with guides to four walks, ranging from a ¾-mile walk around the notch, to a 4-mile two-and-a-half-hour loop to Mt. Norwottuck.

Best Season: Spring through fall; in the winter many of the trails in the Holyoke Range are open for cross-country skiing or snow shoeing.

Length: Varies; there are many trails leading to the summit trails, so you can make this walk as long or as short as you like (you can even drive to the top from May until November). From Halfway House to the summit is ¾ mile; from the picnic area to Taylor's Notch is ½ mile; the Ridge Trail from the summit to the South Hadley town line is 2 miles.

Degree of Difficulty: Easy to moderately difficult.

Highlights: Wonderful views of the winding Connecticut River, the vast plain around Amherst, and picturesque countryside are the rewards of this walk.

Nominator Dick Buegler says that nothing quite compares to the views from the 930-foot summit of Mt. Holyoke, where on a clear day you can see for some 70 miles. Mt. Tom is to the west, and looking that way, you can also see the Connecticut River winding its way along the valley floor. Mt. Greylock is to the northwest and Mount Ascutney, in Vermont, can be seen to the north. There are shady areas for picnicking at the top, and Dick says there is always a nice, cool breeze.

Many people agree with Dick about the beauty of the Holyoke Range. The celebrated opera singer Jenny Lind proclaimed the region and the view from Mt. Holyoke "the Paradise of America."

In addition to beautiful panoramic vistas, you'll also enjoy an upclose look at a variety of wildlife on this walk, including migrating hawks. The best time of year to see the hawks is in the spring when winds from the south help them on their flight northward. One of the best viewing spots is from the Summit House on Mt. Holyoke. Restoration of the Summit House, which began as a Mountain House Inn in 1821, is currently under way. Much of the building was destroyed in 1938 when a hurricane roared through the area.

Trails and dirt roads crisscross the entire Mt. Holyoke Range making it a wonderful place to walk for miles and miles. Dick Buegler particularly likes to hike to the top of Mt. Norwottuck near the eastern end of the range. Norwottuck is the tallest mountain in the range at 1,106 feet; the vertical rise from the valley floor to the ridgeline averages about 800 feet. If you do plan to hike the various roads and trails in the Holyoke Range State Park, remember that some of them cross private property. Please respect landowners' rights. Camping is not allowed anywhere in the park, and fires are permitted only within the picnic area fireplaces on Mt. Holyoke's summit. For current information regarding park hours and weather conditions, call (413) 586-0350.

WESTERN MASSACHUSETTS

Pike's Pond Trail (51)

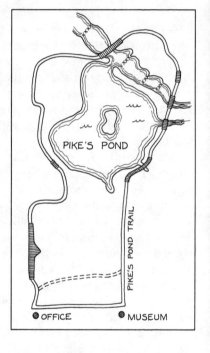

PIKE'S POND

PIKE'S POND TRAIL

OFFICE   MUSEUM

Directions: Pike's Pond is located in the Berkshires at Pleasant Valley Wildlife Sanctuary. From Routes 7 and 20 in Lenox, drive 3 miles north to West Dugway Road on your left. Follow signs to the sanctuary entrance, 1.6 miles away.

Best Season: This is a winter walk, but the sanctuary is wonderful year-round.

Length: ½ mile. Allow about a half to three-quarters of an hour.

Degree of Difficulty: Easy.

Highlights: It may sometimes seem that in New England, nature sleeps in winter. This walk around Pike's Pond allows you to see just how much is really going on, despite the snow and ice.

Before you even begin your walk around Pike's Pond, nominator Cecily Mills suggests you stop in at the office for information on the 7 miles of trails within the sanctuary. "I have taken picnics and wandered throughout the sanctuary during the warmer months," Cecily says. "But it was only after cross-country skiing that I realized a whole other world existed in winter."

Pike's Pond was created when a dam was constructed in 1920, and in 1932 beavers were introduced. As you begin your walk, you can see the beaver dams to the right, up Yokun Brook. Listen for the cracking ice that indicates temperature changes and remember that, though you cannot see them, fish are actively going about their business beneath the ice, as are the beaver. If the pond is not completely frozen, you will see their sleek heads surfacing through the icy water.

The observant walker will notice that the tips of the trees in the hemlock forest are bending to the southeast, away from the prevailing wind. The line of large trees, Cecily explains, are sugar maples, and the sap is already beginning to run in February. The twigs of the yellow birch taste like wintergreen, and Cecily tells us that the neat rows of holes in the apple tree were made by the yellow-bellied sapsucker.

"The first things that I saw on my winter walk," Cecily remembers, "were brilliant flashes of red and blue as the cardinals and blue jays rushed back and forth to the feeder. The cardinals whistled to each other, while the jays cried raucously. By being very quiet, I had the wonderful experience of seeing two ruffled grouse break from cover with a whir of wings, and I watched as a wild turkey stalked across a field. I've had occasional sightings of hawks, but I've always had a difficult time identifying them. In the stillness, I've heard the contrasting sounds of woodpeckers hammering and mourning doves cooing. I have identified over fifty birds in the sanctuary in the summer, but only fifteen on my winter walk. I still dream about spotting an owl or the very rare bald eagle."

For further information about the trails in the sanctuary, write the Berkshire Visitors' Bureau, Berkshire Common, Pittsfield, MA 01201, or call (413) 443-9186.

WESTERN MASSACHUSETTS

South Taconic Trail and Bash Bish Falls (52)

Directions: This walk actually begins in New York State. From New York's Taconic State Parkway, take Route 22 north to Route 344. Watch for signs to the Lower Bash Bish Falls parking lot, just off Route 344.

Best Season: Mid-October for the foliage; spring (after the snow melts) is the most exciting time to see the falls.

Length: 8 miles round-trip. Allow a full day.

Degree of Difficulty: Moderate; wear good hiking shoes and carry water.

Highlights: This wonderful day-long hike combines many of the ingredients that make a walk "great."

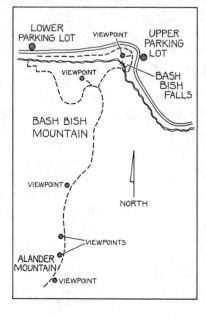

This walk, nominated by Bob Marshall, combines many of the ingredients that make a walk "great"—beautiful scenery, wonderful views, a brook, a hemlock forest, two mountain summits, and Bash Bish Falls—which many people consider to be the most exciting waterfall in Massachusetts. According to legend, a childless Indian maiden, rejected by her husband, jumped into the water at Bash Bish Falls to join her mother, a witch, who lived there.

From the Lower Bash Bish Falls parking lot in New York, you have a choice of two trails, one marked with white paint blazes, the other with blue. Both these trails converge on Bash Bish Mountain in Massachusetts, but the blue-blazed path requires a fording of Bash Bish Brook just above the falls, and this can be tricky when the water is high. The white path crosses a bridge, about 1 mile below the falls, thus avoiding the necessity of fording the brook, but it misses both Bash Bish Falls and the spectacular gorge.

If you decide to take the white-blazed trail, you will discover that it descends an embankment to a road, and quickly crosses the bridge over Bash Bish Brook. Then it leaves the road, making a sharp right, and gradually climbs the lower slopes of Bash Bish Mountain. Near the Massachusetts border, there is a short side trail on the left which leads to a beautiful viewpoint looking westward. From this spot the main trail soon enters Massachusetts and joins the blue trail.

If you decide on the blue trail, follow the north bank of the Bash Bish Brook. Before long you'll be in Massachusetts. Listen for the sound of the falls which are not too far away (the name *Bash Bish* comes from an Indian word meaning the "sound of running water"). When you reach the falls, ascend the steep trail through a hemlock forest to the upper parking lot, where you'll find a short side trail on the right leading to a viewpoint. From here, the main trail descends a short distance along a road to the north bank of the Bash Bish Brook; this is the place where the ford is necessary. Once across, follow the trail west along the south bank of the brook until you reach the top of the falls. The trail now climbs even higher above the gorge, where you'll have the most wonderful views of the cascading water below. You'll want to spend some time here.

Once you've had your fill of the view, follow the trail up through ancient stands of hemlock until it joins the white trail. From here you have another choice to make. According to Bob, "You can turn right on the white trail and return to the parking lot, or turn left on the white trail for a longer hike along the upper pine-covered ridges of Bash Bish Mountain. The trail ascends more gradually now and then proceeds south along the crest of the ridge where there are beautiful views of the valley far below. The farther you go, the more spectacular the vistas get, until at last you reach your goal—the splendid open summits of Alander Mountain—in time, one would hope, for a lunch and a well-earned rest before the long hike back."

WESTERN MASSACHUSETTS

Hiking Up Mt. Greylock (53)

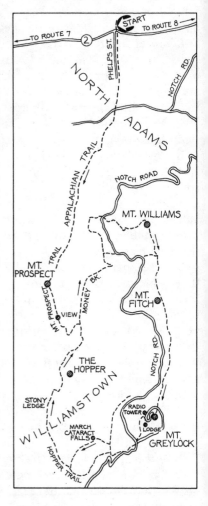

Directions: Elissa Silvio, who nominated this walk, suggests setting up a car shuttle before hiking Mt. Greylock, which is in the northwest corner of Massachusetts, near the town of North Adams. She leaves one car at the summit which is reached by taking Route 2 from North Adams to Notch Road. The other car remains in North Adams, where the walk begins. Park at the school parking lot off Route 2 and Phelps Street.

Best Season: May and June; September and October. Auto road is open from May 15 through October 31.

Length: 6.4 miles. Allow about five or six hours.

Degree of Difficulty: Moderately difficult to difficult. Elevation reaches 3,491 feet. Elevation gain is 2,941 feet.

Highlights: A 360-degree view from the highest peak in Massachusetts.

According to nominator Elissa Silvio, this 6-mile section of the Appalachian Trail is a "walking jewel—the best walk in Massachusetts." Appalachian Trail restrictions apply to this walk: Limit your group to ten people; camp only at designated camping zones and shelters; make no open fires.

From Phelps Street in North Adams, follow the white 2 × 4 inch rectangular blazes that mark the Appalachian Trail (AT), south. At the end of Phelps Street, follow a steep private drive, then veer away from the house, down to a small brook. Cross the brook, and follow the white blazes across a dirt road and another brook. At 1,200 feet, you'll enter a hemlock forest (Mt. Greylock Reservation Boundary) and begin a steep climb up the shoulder of Mt. Prospect. After about 1 mile, you'll get a vista of the Williamstown area to the northwest; then you'll veer east. The trail crosses Notch Road and climbs up Mt. Williams and along the ridge to Mt. Fitch. In the spring you'll enjoy the sight of a profusion of mountain laurel and wildflowers, including lady's slipper orchids, and you'll spot deer, porcupine, and occasionally black bear, hawks, and owls at night. If you're hiking in August, stop to nibble on the raspberries that grow along the trail. "At just about any time of year, you'll meet up with Appalachian Trail 'through hikers,'" Elissa says. "Their stories are as interesting as the views are spectacular."

There are many magnificent viewpoints along this walk, but nothing compares to the summit of Mt. Greylock where, on a clear day, you can see the Catskill and Adirondack mountains of New York State, the Green Mountains of Vermont, and Mt. Monandock of New Hampshire. There's a Memorial Tower at the summit where, during the summer months, park naturalists give lectures every two hours.

The Appalachian Mountain Club manages Bascom Lodge at the summit, where you can find overnight accommodations, meals, and great hospitality. Elissa can vouch for it. "On October 4, 1987," she tells us, "we were hiking this section of the trail and became stranded during an early fall blizzard. The lodge was a true life saver."

Elissa has hiked this trail in all seasons. "I never tire of the views, wildlife, or smells of the forest," she says. "Each trip is a fresh experience."

CENTRAL MASSACHUSETTS

Worcester: God's Acre (54)

Directions: God's Acre is located just outside the downtown area of Worcester. Take Route 122 north from Worcester, and turn left on Chandler Street at Tatnuck Square. Take the first right, Mill Street, and at 200 Mill Street, just before the Mill Swan School, make a sharp right turn on Swan Avenue. Drive up a steep hill, and park where convenient (the road soon deteriorates).

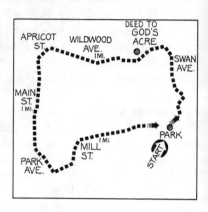

Best Season: Year-round.

Length: About 3 miles.

Degree of Difficulty: Easy to moderate.

Highlights: A unique bit of history is uncovered on this rambling, fun-filled walk.

Without nominator Pearl Towle's description to guide you, it is unlikely that you would ever find God's Acre. It took her awhile to find it herself. "Much has been written about God's Acre in the city of Worcester," Pearl explains, "and I became determined to find it. Success came after many inquiries and explorations. It seems that around 1850, Solomon Parsons decided to set aside an area for the worship of God. He found a huge granite boulder, almost flush with the ground, and had Sylvester Ellis carve on its flat surface a deed to God of some 10 acres of land. The deed contains 219 words, each letter 1½ inches high. How long it took Mr. Ellis to carve it, no one knows. There are no punctuation marks and many misspellings, but here's what the deed says'':

Know all men by these presents that I William G Hall of Worcester in the county of Worcester and Commonwelth of Mass in Consideration of 125 dols paid by the hand of Solomon Parsons of the same Worcester the receipt whereof I do hereby acknowledge do hearby give grant sell and convey unto God through the laws of Jesus Christ which are made known to man by the reckord of the New Testament recorded by Mathew Mark Luke John the Evangelist this land to be governd by the above mentioned laws and togather with the spirit of God the sad tract of land is situated in Worcester above mentioned the south westerly part containing ten acres more or less and bounded as follows viz beginning at the southwest corner of the lot at a stake and stones by land of E Daniels thense easterly by land of S Perry about 37½ rods to a corner of the fence thence northerly by land of L Gates about 54 rods to a corner of the fense thence westerly land of the hears of J Fowler about 24 rods to a chestnut tree in the wall at the corner of the land of said Daniels and a heap of stones by the side of it thence southerly to the bounds first mentioned

"This deed was never recorded in the Registry of Deeds. The area, known as Tatnuck Hill, or Rattlesnake Hill, has now grown to 130 acres. It is obscure and not well cared for, but it is designated by the city as a conservation area. Several rocky hiking trails lead from here to Goddard Industrial Park and the Worcester Municipal Airport."

To reach God's Acre, walk about a ½ mile from your car, going by Passways 4, 5, 6, and Paris Avenue on the left. Pearl advises you to be careful to stay on Swan Avenue because the road has many loops and turns and no markings. Turn right at Pole 42, and walk up a slight grade to Pole 40 and a gas manhole. Up ahead you'll see a chain hanging in a tree. Walk to the left about 25 feet to a path on the right; this leads to the "rock deed," carved by Sylvester Ellis. You can return the same way, or go back via a longer route by retracing your steps to Pole 42 and walking straight, past a residence on the right. After about ½ mile, Swan Avenue joins Wildwood Avenue, a paved street. Go right and walk about 1 mile to 18 Apricot Street. Turn left and walk to Route 9 at 1374 Main Street. Walk left and bear left at the junction of Park Avenue. After about 1 mile, make a left on Mill Street; 1 more mile on Mill Street will bring you back to Swan Avenue and your car.

CENTRAL MASSACHUSETTS

Old Railroad Roadbed Trail (55)

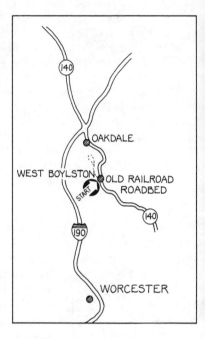

Directions: This walk is located just north of the city of Worcester. From the village of Oakdale, drive south on Route 140 for about 400 feet, and turn right into a parking area.

Best Season: Year-round.

Length: 2¾ miles. Allow about an hour and a quarter for the round-trip.

Degree of Difficulty: Easy; the terrain is flat.

Highlights: This walk is close to a city, yet it affords wonderful views of the river and an opportunity to enjoy the quiet peacefulness of the country.

This walk, nominated by Stanton Whitman, follows an old roadbed of what was once the Massachusetts Central Railroad, along the north bank of the Quinapoxit River in West Boylston. The railroad was abandoned after the devastating hurricane of 1938, and the ties were removed.

From the parking area, walk northwest, by an entrance gate, then follow the old railroad bed along the river. After about ¼ mile, you'll see the Metropolitan District Commission Building at Shaft One. Here a tunnel from the Quabbin Reservoir empties water into the Quinapoxit River. The river then carries the water to the Wachusett Reservoir which serves the city of Boston.

After you've walked for about ½ mile, you'll come to an old mill site on the left (formerly Harrisville), and at about ⅔ mile, there is (or was) a milepost on the right indicating that it is 62 miles to Northampton from this point. After another mile, there's another milepost. Turn around at the old bridge abutment and return.

When you've finished this bucolic walk along the Quinapoxit, you may want to spend a little time in Worcester, which is the geographic center of Massachusetts. Settled in 1673, the area had a somewhat turbulent beginning, first as the site of Indian attacks and then as a scene for fighting during Shay's Rebellion. In 1786 and 1787, Daniel Shay, a soldier in the Revolutionary War, led a group of economically depressed farmers in an armed revolt which was eventually dispersed by state troops.

In 1822, a canal system was established on the Blackstone River which runs through Worcester, and the city enjoyed a period of rapid industrialization. Today it is a manufacturing center for metals, machinery, textiles, precision instruments, chemicals, and pharmaceuticals.

In contrast to the industrial part of the city is the 51-acre Quinsigamond State Park, where you can enjoy camping, picnicking, boating, fishing, and swimming. The park office is located at 10 North Lake Avenue in Worcester.

CENTRAL MASSACHUSETTS

Mt. Watatic Loop (56)

Directions: This walk begins in Ashburnham, just off Route 119 in northern Massachusetts. From Worcester take Route 190 north to Route 2, then head west to Route 101 near Gardner. Drive north on 101, through Ashburnham, to Route 119. The Mt. Watatic Trailhead parking area is about 1¼ miles west of the junction of Routes 101 and 119.

Best Season: Spring through fall, but a nice day in winter can also be good.

Length: 3 miles. Allow about two and a half hours.

Degree of Difficulty: Moderate; it's uphill to the top.

Highlights: This walk through the woods on a low mountain offers wonderful views with only a moderate challenge.

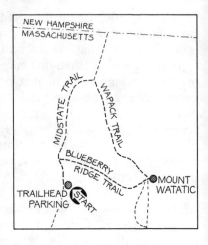

Mt. Watatic is the northern terminus of the Midstate Trail, which crisscrosses Massachusetts from its southern terminus on the Rhode Island border to Mt. Watatic, just south of New Hampshire—a total distance of 85 miles. The entire trail has been blazed with yellow triangles, making it easy to follow, and most of the sections are easily accessible from town roads or highways.

This particular section, which includes a hike to the summit of Mt. Watatic, was nominated by Stanton Whitman, secretary of the Midstate Trail Committee. From the parking area off Route 119, follow the yellow triangles that mark the Midstate Trail uphill for about 1¼ miles to the New Hampshire state line. Here you'll find a granite monument marking the corner where three towns come together: Ashburnham and Ashby, Massachusetts, and New Ipswich, New Hampshire.

From this point, turn right and walk east along a stone wall for about 230 feet to the Wapack Trail, also marked with yellow triangles. Follow the Wapack Trail up to the top of the 1,832-foot Mt. Watatic. All along the way you'll have wonderful views, but it's hard to beat the ones from the summit. There's a fire tower you can climb to see even farther.

For the return trip, descend and turn right, past a small shelter, onto the Blueberry Ridge Trail, which is blazed with blue markers. The Blueberry Ridge Trail intersects the Midstate Trail where you can turn left to return to the parking area.

EASTERN NEW HAMPSHIRE

Wolfeboro: Three Walks (57)

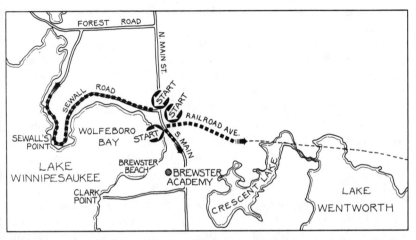

Directions: Wolfeboro is located near the southeastern corner of Lake Winnipesaukee at the juncture of Routes 109, 28, and 109A. All three walks start within about ¼ mile of each other in the downtown area of the village. Nominator Steve Flagg of the Nordic Skier, 19 N. Main Street, says to stop into the store for information on other hiking and bicycling routes in the area. The store is open seven days a week.

Best Season: Spring, summer, fall.

Length: The longest of these walks is a 4-mile loop along the edge of Lake Winnipesaukee. The other two walks are under 2 miles each.

Degree of Difficulty: Easy.

Highlights: A chance to explore the quaint charm of one of New England's most beautiful picture-postcard villages.

Lake Winnipesaukee is the largest lake in New Hampshire and a favorite spot for summer vacationing. In fact, Wolfeboro, one of the most charming of all the villages on the lake, is known as "America's Oldest Summer Resort." Officers of the Revolutionary Army loved to visit Wolfeboro, and John Wentworth, the last colonial governor of New Hampshire, summered there. "It's the most beautiful town to drive into," says Steve Flagg, who nominated three walks in Wolfeboro. "It rises up on a hill from the water and looks just like a postcard."

Steve's first walk begins at the Railroad Station on Railroad Avenue in the heart of downtown Wolfeboro. "The station's a beautiful structure," Steve says, "which was renovated in 1987 after lightning struck it." Follow the railroad track along the river, and after a mile or two you'll come to two interconnected lakes: Crescent and Wentworth. At that point Steve says you can return or continue on for more spectacular views of Lake Wentworth.

The second walk is a 4-mile loop which starts at Sewall Road and follows the southeastern shore of Lake Winnipesaukee—a section known as Wolfeboro Bay. The road is tree-shaded, and you'll pass by some magnificent old homes. Take Forest Road and then N. Main to loop back to the start. This walk gives you wonderful views of the lake, and in the distance you can see the Belknap Mountain Range.

The third walk leads from town to Brewster Beach on Lake Winnipesaukee, where there is public access for swimming. Take S. Main Street to Clark Road. It's about 1.5 miles to the beach. Along the way you'll pass by Brewster Academy, a private school established in 1887, and Clark House, which goes all the way back to around 1778. Clark House is furnished with eighteenth-century artifacts and is open to the public. Nearby is an old schoolhouse and a replica of an old fire station.

For a surprising bit of "Hollywood in New Hampshire," you may want to drive north on Route 109 to the Castle in the Clouds, the dream come true of Thomas Gustave Plant, who bought 6,000 acres of wilderness and imported workmen from Europe to create a castle from which he could see beauty wherever he looked. Today you can enjoy Plant's fantasy, which is set high in the Ossipee Mountain Range and affords spectacular views of Lake Winnipesaukee and the White Mountains. The ponds, gardens, and waterfalls surrounding the castle make it a wonderful place to explore on foot. It's open from May to mid-October.

SOUTHEASTERN NEW HAMPSHIRE

Discovering Manchester (58)

Directions: Manchester is about 53 miles north of Boston off Route 93. Stop in at the Manchester Historic Association, 129 Amherst Street, for your Historic Trail Map. The association is open Tuesdays through Fridays from 9 a.m. to 4 p.m. and Saturdays from 10 a.m. to 4 p.m.

Best Season: Nominator Fred Matuszewski likes this walk best in the fall, but he says winter is also good because you can see the architectural diversity without leaves blocking your view!

Length: About 5 miles, but allow at least half a day to "discover" Manchester.

Degree of Difficulty: Easy.

Highlights: This walk through Manchester, a town planned by a textile manufacturing company, gives a glimpse into working conditions in the late nineteenth century. More importantly, however, it shows what dedicated citizens can do when their hometown is threatened.

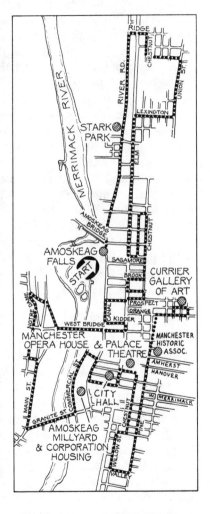

This walk, nominated by Fred Matuszewski, begins at the Manchester Historic Association at the corner of Pine and Amherst.

Stop inside for a look at a collection of antique fire-fighting equipment, old books and manuscripts relating to Manchester's history, photographs, and family records. Here you can pick up a self-guided Historic Trail Map which describes various points of interest in Manchester and provides information of historic, economic, cultural, and architectural significance.

The first stop on the tour is Amoskeag Falls on the Merrimack River, an important source of fish for the Indians and early settlers. At the east end of the falls (now hidden by a power dam) is the site where Archibald Stark, father of Revolutionary War hero John Stark, built his home to protect the fishing rights of white settlers in New Hampshire from Massachusetts poachers. The house was moved to Elm Street (No. 2000) in 1970. Maintained by the Daughters of the American Revolution, you can visit Stark House from May 15 to October 15 on Wednesdays and Sundays from 1:30 to 4:30 p.m.

The walk continues up River Road to Stark Park where a statue of John Stark, hero of the Battles of Bunker Hill and Bennington dominates the crest of the hill. From here you can look down on the Merrimack and view the Uncanoonuc Mountains in the distance. Also in the park are the graves of Stark and his family. His wife Molly was immortalized in Stark's rallying cry at the Battle of Bennington: "There are the Redcoats, and they will be ours, or tonight Molly Stark sleeps a widow."

You will get some historical perspective on Manchester's early beginnings as an industrial center when you pass by the Amoskeag Millyard and Corporation Housing. The Amoskeag Manufacturing Company began in 1830 on the west bank of the Merrimack and grew to become the largest textile mill in the world, producing more than a mile of cotton cloth each minute at its peak in the last half of the nineteenth century. The Depression marked the end of the company, which closed its doors on Christmas Eve, 1935, but not the end of the town it had created. Citizens of Manchester, determined that the city would survive, formed a committee to raise money in order to purchase the Amoskeag buildings and attract new industries. As you can see, their efforts were successful: Today Manchester not only survives, it thrives!

As you continue this walk through Manchester, you will discover a variety of architecture, including two homes designed by Frank Lloyd Wright, a number of fine old Victorian homes, an Italianate mansion built in the 1880s, the Gothic City Hall, and the beautiful Manchester Opera House, which was considered "the most elegant pleasure palace north of Boston" when it was built in 1881. Other cultural features along this walk include the Palace Theatre at 83 Hanover Street. Built in the heyday of vaudeville, the theater was restored in 1974 and is now operated by the New Hampshire Performing Arts Center, which offers more than a hundred performances a year, from Shakespeare to musical comedy, from symphonies to bluegrass. And you won't want to miss a visit to the Currier Gallery of Art at 192 Orange Street, which contains one of New England's finest collections of European art from the fourteenth century to the present. The beautiful Renaissance building was the home of Moody Currier, governor of New Hampshire from 1885 to 1887. The Currier Gallery of Art is open Tuesday through Saturday from 10 a.m. to 4 p.m. and Sunday from 2 to 5 p.m.

SOUTHEASTERN NEW HAMPSHIRE

Massabesic Lake (59)

Directions: The walk is located in the city of Manchester, about 53 miles north of Boston. Take Route I-93 to Candia Road Circle where you can follow signs to the Massabesic Lake Trailhead.

Best Season: Late spring to early winter.

Length: About 4 miles. Allow four and a half to five hours.

Degree of Difficulty: Easy; the trail is paved with wood chips. Elevation changes are never more than 20 feet.

Highlights: This scenic, country walk right in the middle of Manchester makes a great getaway spot.

Manchester is perhaps best known for its historical significance as the home of the world's largest textile producer. Near the end of the nineteenth century, the Amoskeag Manufacturing Company em

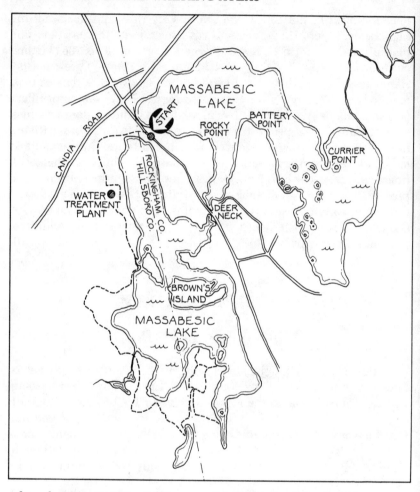

ployed some 15,000 people, one-third of Manchester's work force. When the company folded during the Depression, a citizens group, determined that Manchester would never again be so reliant on one industry that its demise would threaten the city's very existence, set out to attract a variety of businesses to the city. Today their efforts are reflected in the vibrant diversity of New Hampshire's largest city.

This walk, nominated by Clem Lemire, affords an opportunity to see another side of Manchester, one that visitors usually miss. It is a side of the city that reaches back to a time long before the Amoskeag Manufacturing Company came into being and long before any buildings were constructed along the Merrimack. It reaches back to the time when Indians came each year to fish in the area (in fact, the word *amoskeag* is an Algonkian Indian word meaning "place of many fish") and to enjoy the beauty of this place. They held great feasts, played games, fished, concluded treaties, and gathered in tribal ceremonies. On this walk, you will feel that you are in another time. Instead of buildings, you will find trees; instead of honking horns, you will hear the sounds of birds; and instead of the Merrimack River, source of the power that fueled the textile industry, you will look down on peaceful Massabesic Lake, enjoyed solely for the beauty and diversion it provides, just as the Indians enjoyed the rivers and lakes tens of thousands of years ago. This walk transports you instantly from a city to a country environment. From the time you leave your car in the parking lot on Candia Road Circle, it is under a minute to the woods, where you'll be walking amid trees with birds darting all around you. In the spring you'll be surrounded by flowers, and from almost every spot along the trail, you'll have a beautiful view of the lake.

"This trail is a favorite of several local walking groups," Clem says, "and is enjoyed by many of the people who live and work in Manchester. So, in addition to its natural woodsy setting and clear views of the lake, it is also a perfect place to meet and have fun with friends. Even the parking lot where the walk begins is an outstandingly beautiful spot. You will see the wide open waters and the Sailboating Club to the right. Across the road is one of the best junior baseball complexes on the east coast. Along the walk you will also see the area of Manchester's beautiful and modern water treatment plant, which has won national awards." And Clem assures us that, although the trail is well known in the community, it is never too crowded.

SOUTHEASTERN NEW HAMPSHIRE

Portsmouth: A Visit to the Past (60)

Directions: Located on the Piscataqua River, which flows here into the Atlantic Ocean, Portsmouth is New Hampshire's only seaport. It is accessible from I-95, north or south (the New Hampshire or Maine turnpikes). Take exit 7, and follow Market Street to Hanover Street.

Turn right on Hanover to the Hanover Street Garage, where there is always ample parking.

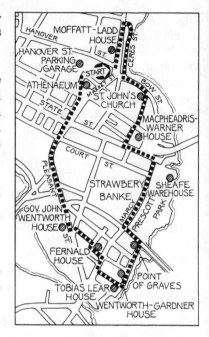

Best Season: Year-round; the coastal climate makes Portsmouth pleasant in any season, though a midwinter walk may be bracing, with temperatures in the twenties (°F).

Length: About 1 mile. Allow at least an hour.

Degree of Difficulty: Easy.

Highlights: This is a walk into the past; Portsmouth was settled in the 1600s and retains much of its historic flavor.

This walk takes you along some of the oldest and most historic streets of New England. It begins on the banks of the Piscataqua River where the first Portsmouth settlers landed in 1630, and passes by buildings that are older than two centuries. Nominator Jim Garvin expresses it perfectly when he says: "To take this walk is to be transported back in time, not strictly in the imagination, but also in reality. The city and its companion river conspire to conjure up backwaters and eddies in the stream of time, places where one's senses are so immersed in the past it's as if one had really been set down in another time and place."

From the parking garage, proceed north along Market Street. On your right is Merchant's Row, a series of twelve connected mercantile buildings constructed after a devastating fire in 1802. Just beyond Merchant's Row, on the left, is the Moffatt-Ladd House, one of the grandest Georgian mansions in New England. Built in 1763, it is now owned by the Society of the Colonial Dames of America and is open to the public.

Descend the stairs in front of the Moffatt-Ladd House, and head for the riverbank; you can see the town of Kittery, Maine, on the opposite shore. Turn right (south) along Ceres Street, which was formerly a back alley serving the lower floors of the buildings on Merchant's Row. Today the old warehouses and shops have been converted into modern stores and restaurants. On your left, where the river eddies in a small cove, are the tugboats of the Portsmouth Navigation Company, where Jim Garvin says you may meet some of the skilled crews who pilot large ocean-going freighters, oil tankers, and salt boats up the winding channel of the Piscataqua. "Here, too," Jim says, "you may find Bobbie McLane, night watchman for the tugboat company and resident of the Ceres Street area for more than thirty years. With a bit of prompting, Bob will recount the days when this entire waterfront was derelict, the buildings along Merchant's Row largely empty, and the hustle and bustle of the present day merely a hope for the future."

When you reach Bow Street, turn left and walk up a winding hill to Chapel Street and the brick St. John's Church. Built after the fire of 1806 destroyed its predecessor, St. John's is surrounded by a walled graveyard filled with the tombs of the elite of colonial days. The church is one of the earliest surviving designs by Alexander Parris, who later achieved fame as a leading architect in Boston. Enter St. John's by the right-hand (southern) door; in the entry you may see a loaf of bread, left there daily for any poor person who might need it—a bequest made in 1779 by Theodore Atkinson, Secretary of the Province of New Hampshire. Inside the church are many relics of colonial days, including one of only a few "Vinegar" Bibles, so named for a typographical error in the Parable of the Vineyards.

From St. John's, walk south along Chapel Street to the corner of Daniel Street. On your left is the Macpheadris-Warner House, which was built in 1716. Inside are splendid examples of furniture made by Portsmouth artisans and several portraits by the fashionable English painter Joseph Blackburn, who was a resident of Portsmouth for a brief time.

Continue along Chapel Street to State Street and turn left, toward the river. Near the end of Memorial Bridge, turn right onto Marcy Street; beautiful Prescott Park will be on your left. At the point where Marcy Street narrows, you will begin to see the buildings of Strawbery Banke, an outdoor museum, on your right. Named for the original colony (which was called Strawbery Banke because of the strawberries the colonists found here), this restoration includes nearly thirty buildings, ranging in date from the late 1600s to the early 1800s, as well as several craft shops and exhibits.

Opposite Strawbery Banke on Marcy Street is the Portsmouth Heritage Museum, a brick building constructed in the 1830s to house the office and counting room of the Portsmouth Marine Railway. Today the building contains exhibits of memorabilia and art depicting the history of Portsmouth. Beyond the museum is the Liberty Pole, a tall wooden flagpole which stands on the same site as one erected in 1766 to protest the hated Stamp Act.

On the seawall at the far end of Prescott Park is the Sheafe Warehouse, possibly dating from 1705. The overhang on the end of the building was used to hoist goods off the decks of gundalows, a local type of rivercraft. Legend states that John Paul Jones' Revolutionary flagship, *Ranger*, was outfitted at this warehouse.

At the southern end of Prescott Park, at the junction of Mechanic Street and the bridge to nearby Pierce Island, is the Point of Graves, Portsmouth's oldest cemetery. With stones dating back to the 1680s, this graveyard offers a sampler of the various winged skulls, cherubs, and coats of arms which were popular in eighteenth-century mortuary art.

Walk south now along Mechanic Street, and follow the waterfront. To your right, extending away from the river, are several narrow streets crowded with small wooden houses; this part of Portsmouth, untouched by fire, remains as it was in the 1700s. On your right, at the corner of Mechanic and Gardner streets, is the Wentworth-Gardner House, which was built around 1760 and is another of the great Georgian mansions of New England. Just around the corner, on Hunking Street, is the Tobias Lear House, birthplace of George Washington's private secretary.

Continue west on Hunking Street to Marcy Street, and turn right. Cross Meeting House Hill at the South Meeting House, now the Portsmouth Children's Museum. Diagonally behind the South Meeting House is the old gambrel-roofed Fernald House, part of which dates back to the late 1600s. Turn left here, and walk along Howard Street to Pleasant Street. Across from the intersection of Howard and Pleasant streets stands the Governor John Wentworth House, the Portsmouth home of New Hampshire's last royal governor. Wentworth considered this dwelling merely a "little hut," preferring to spend his time (and money) in a mansion on the shores of a pond 50 miles inland.

Walk north (right) along Pleasant Street, and note how the houses assume an increasingly imposing appearance as you approach the center of town. Visible at the end of Pleasant Street is a long row of brick buildings constructed after the fire of 1802. The tallest is the Portsmouth Athenaeum, a private library and museum, open to the public during restricted hours. At the left (west) of the Athenaeum Block, turn right on High Street, and walk straight ahead to the Hanover Street Garage, where the walk began.

SOUTHEASTERN NEW HAMPSHIRE

Exeter: String Bridge Walking Tour (61)

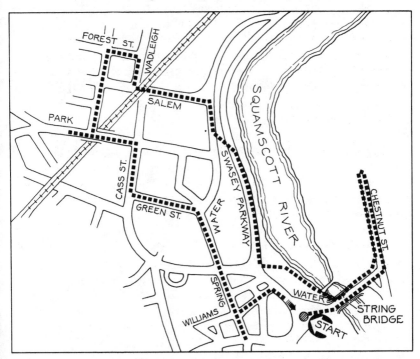

Directions: Exeter is located in the southeast corner of New Hampshire. From I-95, take Highway 101 to Route 108. This walk begins at the Water Street parking lot on the corner of Williams and Water streets.

Best Season: June through September.

Length: The walk is only about 2½ miles, but there's lots to do and see in Exeter; plan on about half a day.

Degree of Difficulty: Easy.

Highlights: This is a peaceful walk in the footsteps of a not-so-peaceful history.

This walk is based on a self-guided tour brochure called *Four Walking Tours of Exeter, New Hampshire.* For a copy, stop by The Exeter Area Chamber of Commerce, 120 Water Street, or call (603) 772-2411. What follows are just some of the highlights from the detailed walking tour.

This particular walk is named for the String Bridge you'll cross at the beginning of the walk. From the parking area, walk toward the river to the bridge, called *String* because at one time it was a single log, or "stringer." Cross the bridge and turn right on Chestnut Street, where there are a number of interesting old buildings. Note especially 5 Chestnut Street, which is the site of a jail where Tories were incarcerated during revolutionary times. If you'd been here then, you might also have seen a few counterfeiters in the jail, or perhaps some deserters from the Continental Army. The red brick building at 11 Chestnut was probably built around 1830. It belonged to the Exeter Manufacturing Co. before becoming the home of Hervey Kent, an agent for the mill.

Follow the river path behind the Water Street stores (accessible between the Janvrin Block and the Wood Block), and proceed to the Ladd-Gilman House on Governor's Lane, now known as Cincinnati Memorial Hall. This was once a small, square brick building, constructed around 1721 by Nathaniel Ladd. In 1752, Daniel Gilman purchased the eastern half of the house for his son, Nicholas. An addition toward Water Street was added, and the structure was clapboarded over to make it look like one unit. Members of the Gilman family played important roles in both state and national politics. Nicholas was state treasurer during the Revolutionary War; his son John was governor of New Hampshire for a total of fourteen one-year terms; another son, Nicholas, Jr., was one of the signers of the Constitution; and a third son, Nathaniel, represented Exeter in the state legislature.

Walk now to Swasey Parkway, designed by the Olmsted Brothers of Brookline, Massachusetts, and completed in 1931—a gift to Exeter from Ambrose Swasey. Across the river you can see the Powder House, where some of the powder captured during the raids of Fort William and Mary, in New Castle, New Hampshire, in December 1774, was stored. Continue along Swasey Parkway, walking left on Salem Street, then right on Wadleigh, and left again on Forest. The building at 9 Forest Street was constructed in 1870 as a jail to replace the one on Chestnut Street. Still referred to as "The Old Jail," it has been converted to apartments. Turn left now, and walk across Salem to Park Street. The crystal clear waters from the spring you'll pass have been enjoyed by residents of Exeter almost from the beginning of the town's settlement.

The house at 47 Park Street was moved from Center Street in 1790. It belonged to Deacon John Rice and was one of eleven homes in Exeter where gunpowder was hidden temporarily after the raids on Fort William and Mary. Later the house became the parsonage for the First Church. The square building at 51 Park Street was the old Exeter Bank, originally located on Center and Water streets. It was at this bank, in 1828, that the great bank robbery took place. Thirty thousand dollars was taken; all of it later recovered.

Giddinge's Tavern, built in 1723, is located at 37 Park Street. Many travelers quenched their thirst here, especially the loggers who brought the large pines for His Majesty's Navy down to the river. Walk right on Cass Street and stop at No. 25, the Odiorne-Bickford House. Built around 1723 by Major John Gilman, the house was used by his daughter Joanna and her husband, Deacon Thomas Odiorne. This house is another of the Exeter homes used to store gunpowder during the revolution. It is also believed that this home was one of the stops on the Underground Railroad. A left turn on Green Street will bring you to Deacon Odiorne's Duck Manufactory (No. 18), where some of the finest sailcloth in New Hampshire was produced.

Turn right now on Water Street, and stop by No. 253, where from 1770 to 1838, Dr. Joseph Tilton lived. Dr. Tilton, who visited his patients on horseback, carrying medicine in his saddlebags, lived to the age of 93. Continue down Water Street to Spring Street, where at No. 21 you can see the old Folsom Tavern, moved from the Square (now a Mobil Station) in 1729. George Washington was at this tavern in 1789, stopping by on his way from Portsmouth to Haverhill.

Turn left on Williams Street, and note the brick house on the corner of Williams Court and Ladd's Lane. The bindery for the Williams Brothers Publishing Business, which at one time printed some 50,000 books annually, is attached to the ell of this building. The house was later owned by Dr. Abner L. Merrill and then by Henry Anderson, for whom it is named. Anderson owned several schooners which used to come up the Squamscott River to dock at the wharves behind the McReel Block.

Continuing down Williams Street, you'll come again to Water Street and the Water Street parking lot. Before leaving, you may want to ponder a little more history. In 1734, colonists dressed as Indians (they had changed at Giddinge's Tavern on Park Street) came to this site and bodily removed the King's men who had come to inspect the forests to make sure no trees were being "illegally" cut. The Exeter "Indians" sculled the ships belonging to the inspectors and destroyed the sails; the King's men had no choice but to get back to Portsmouth as best they could (probably on foot).

CENTRAL NEW HAMPSHIRE

Point Trail and Lakeside Trail Loop (62)

Directions: The walk is located in the Paradise Point Nature Center, Hebron. From Concord, take I-93 north to exit 23, and follow Route 104 west to Bristol. At Bristol, take 3A north, and follow the shoreline of Newfound Lake to North Shore Road. Turn left on North Shore, and drive 1 mile to the Nature Center. There is a $1 fee for nonmembers; 50¢ for children.

Best Season: Summer; the Nature Center is open from 10 a.m. to 5 p.m. daily, from late June to Labor Day.

Length: Under a mile. Allow about an hour.

Degree of Difficulty: Easy.

Highlights: This scenic nature walk takes you out onto a peninsula in Newfound Lake where you can sit at the water's edge and enjoy views of the surrounding mountains.

Five self-guiding trails wind through the Paradise Point Nature Center, which borders beautiful Newfound Lake. Nominator Margot Iwan particularly likes to combine the Point Trail and the Lakeside Trail. The two meet at Paradise Point, a peninsula that juts out into the lake and gives you a sensational "six-mile" view.

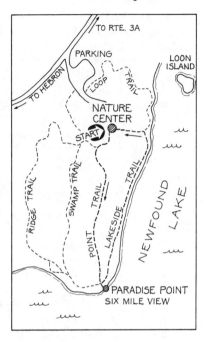

The Trailhead for the Point Trail is just outside the Nature Center. You'll pass through a lush green hemlock forest where a thick carpet of moss grows in the swamp. A few squirrels and chipmunks will probably accompany you along the trail, and you'll see and hear plenty of birds. Margot says there are also some interesting natural phenomena to note along the route, including a tree sitting on top of its roots, which are about three feet above ground, and provide an unusual sort of "chair" for the tree's trunk.

When you reach the juncture of the two trails, walk out onto Paradise Point for wonderful vistas of the lake and surrounding mountains. You won't want to leave this place.

For the return trip, follow the Lakeside Trail along the shore of the lake and back to the Nature Center, where you can view special exhibits of plants and animals, and displays of natural history and environmental issues. Naturalists are available for guided tours or special programs; for more information, write Paradise Point Nature Center, North Shore Road, Hebron, New Hampshire 03232, or call (603) 744-3516.

Visitors are asked not to "collect or disturb any plants, animals, or rocks in the sanctuary," and on the back of the trail map, you'll find an anecdote story told by naturalist Loren Eisley, which seems so appropriate, we reprint it here:

There is a story about one of our great atomic physicists—a story for whose authenticity I cannot vouch, and therefore I will not mention his name—this man, one of the chief architects of the atomic bomb, so the story runs, was out wandering in the woods one day with a friend when he came upon a small tortoise. Overcome with pleasurable excitement, he took up the tortoise and started home, thinking to surprise his children with it. After a few steps he paused and surveyed the tortoise doubtfully. "What's the matter?" asked his friend. Without responding, the great scientist slowly retraced his steps as precisely as possible, and gently set the turtle down on the exact spot from which he had taken him up. Then he turned solemnly to his friend. "It just struck me," he said, "that perhaps, for one man, I have tampered enough with the universe." He turned, and left the turtle to wander on its way.

CENTRAL NEW HAMPSHIRE

New Hampshire Winery (63)

Directions: The winery is located in Laconia. From Concord, take I-93 north to exit 20. Follow Route 3 east to Route 107 south, and watch for signs to New Hampshire Winery.

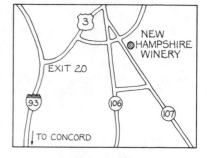

Best Season: Summer and fall; the winery is open daily from 11 a.m. to 4 p.m., June through October.

Length: Not far; this is a long walk back in history, but it requires very little footwork.

Degree of Difficulty: Easy.

Highlights: On this walk you'll tour New Hampshire's only winery, taste some unique beverages, and maybe even meet the Howard brothers, Roger, Pete, and Aldie, who are doing some pretty exciting and unusual things with wine.

Have you ever heard of Switchel? How about Rock Maple Liqueur? If so, chances are you've heard of the New Hampshire Winery, the first winery in New England and the only one in New Hampshire. "Grapes are tough to grow here," says Aldie Howard, who with his brothers, Pete and Roger, purchased the winery in 1986. "Short season. Bugs. Very cold winter." As a result, the Howards waste nothing and use everything they have. For example, they inherited 2,000 gallons of apple-cider vinegar when they bought the winery, and Aldie thought it might be interesting to make Switchel, a nonalcoholic beverage that was popular during colonial times. He found some old recipes in early-American cookbooks and came up with a blend of water, apple-cider vinegar, molasses, honey, and maple syrup. The result, which has become extremely popular, is sold only at the winery. It can be served hot or cold and is reportedly a "high-energy" beverage. "An eighteenth-century Gatorade," Aldie calls it.

Another popular item at the winery is Rock Maple Liqueur, dedicated to the brothers' great-great grandfather, John Howard, who apparently loved it and left notes about it in the Howard family Bible. Rock Maple Liqueur, with over 40%-pure grade-A maple syrup, is a secret blend known only to the Howards and is available only in New Hampshire state liquor stores.

New Hampshire Winery dates back to 1969 when a retired New York chemist started growing grapes and began the White Mountain Vineyard. The next owners discovered all too quickly what Aldie told us from the start: "Grapes are tough to grow here." They went bankrupt within two years, and the winery was closed for four years until the Howards came along. And they're having fun. In addition to the Rock Maple Liqueur and Switchel, the Howards make apple wine, raspberry wine, elderberry wine, a red and a white table wine, and a new wine called Marechal Foch, which is made from the Marechal Foch grape, a cross between the American Vitis Riparia and the French Gamay and Pinot Noir.

"So," Aldie says in conclusion, "here we are in New Hampshire. Care for a walk?"

CENTRAL NEW HAMPSHIRE

Welch-Dickey Loop Trail (64)

Directions: The walk is located in the Pemigewasset Ranger District of the White Mountain National Forest. From I-93, take exit 28, and head east on Route 49 for about 5 miles. Turn left, cross the bridge, and follow Upper Mad River Road 0.7 mile to Orris Road (you'll see the Welch/Dickey Mountain sign). Turn right on Orris Road, and go 0.6 mile to the parking area.

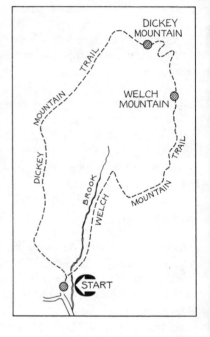

Best Season: Fall is beautiful for the foliage, but you can take the walk year-round, weather permitting.

Length: 4½ miles. Allow about three and a half hours.

Degree of Difficulty: Moderately difficult; the walk is mostly uphill. Be careful on the cliffs, stay on the trail, and carry water.

Highlights: Beautiful views from the summits of Welch and Dickey mountains are the rewards of this walk.

This walk, nominated by Ned Therrien, begins at an elevation of 1,040 feet. From the parking lot, follow the trail for about 15 yards to a fork. Take the right fork, which crosses over a brook and, after about ½ mile, makes a sharp right. From here the trail leads to the ledges on the south ridge of Welch Mountain. You'll pass jack pines and dwarf birches on your way to the 2,605-foot summit of Welch Mountain, and you may see a chipmunk or two and a few squirrels. Ned says you can crawl over or squeeze through the rocks in a few places, which adds a feeling of adventure to the walk. You may want to stop at the summit of Welch Mountain for a while before continuing on to Dickey Mountain. There are very few trees at the top, and the views are excellent. There is also a wonderful wilderness feeling here, making it a good place to let go of the stress and strain of work or city living.

From the Welch Mountain summit, the trail descends steeply to a wooded col and then rises, winding to the left around a high rock slab. Above the rock there is a very short branch trail which leads to an overlook from an open ledge. After taking in the view, continue along the main trail to the 2,734-foot summit of Dickey Mountain. You've gone almost 2½ miles at this point.

There are many outlook ledges as the trail heads down from the Dickey Mountain summit. Don't miss any of them. At the base of one of the ledges, the trail enters the woods and continues down to a logging road. Eventually you'll be back at the parking lot.

If you have time after your walk and want to take a fantastic drive through the White Mountains, head north on I-93 to Lincoln. Here you can pick up the 34-mile Kancamagus (pronounced Kang-ka-MAW-gus) Highway which goes east from Lincoln, following branches of the Pemigewasset River to the Kancamagus Pass, nearly 3,000 feet high (the Kancamagus Highway is the highest mountain highway in the northeast). From this point, the road descends along the Swift River to Conway. This road is steep in places, so drive carefully. There are overlooks along the way where you can stop to enjoy the fabulous views.

CENTRAL NEW HAMPSHIRE

Mt. Cardigan Summit (65)

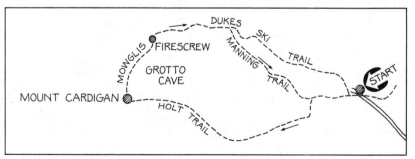

Directions: Mt. Cardigan is located south of the White Mountains between the towns of Orange and Alexandria. Take I-93 to exit 26, and follow Route 104 west (left) to Bristol. Head north on Route 3A, then west at the stone church at the foot of Newfound Lake. After 3.1 miles, bear right and then turn left after 6.3 miles. At 7.4 miles from the church, turn right onto a gravel road. Bear right at the "Red Schoolhouse," and continue to Cardigan Lodge, which is maintained by the Appalachian Mountain Club and provides meals and lodging (there is also a campground and "Hi-Cabin") during the summer season. The road to the lodge is plowed in winter, but must be driven with great care.

Best Season: Summer.

Length: 2 miles. Allow two to three hours.

Degree of Difficulty: Difficult; the last part of the walk is a scramble up bare rock which some say is among the more difficult climbs in New England. There are easier routes to the summit, however.

Highlights: This walk is a challenge, but it's a lot of fun, and the view from the top is fantastic.

This walk up Cardigan Mountain, nominated by Margot Iwan, follows the Elizabeth Holt Trail to the summit, then descends along the Mowglis and Manning trails. From the parking lot, walk along the old logging road to the Trailhead for the Holt Trail. "Don't miss the beautiful pond on the left before the trail," Margot urges, "you might spot a beaver there." The trail is short, but very steep, especially toward the end. You should not attempt it under wet or icy conditions. The trail starts in a deciduous forest and follows a crystal-clear stream, alive with aquatic insects. As the trail climbs, you'll come to spruce and fir trees, and, finally, to a big rock with a crack in it. "This is the first challenge," Margot says. "You have to get up the rock by holding on to the crack."

At the top there is very little vegetation, but you'll find some blueberry patches. If it's the right season and the berries are ripe, they make a wonderful snack. From here you still have a short, steep scramble up the rocks to the summit, where the views are spectacular. "You can see the White Mountains to the north," Margot says, "and the view all around is dotted with beautiful lakes. It's just incredible. You can climb a fire tower and see even more!"

To return, follow the Mowglis Trail past a side trail off to your right (which leads to Grotto Cave) to the top of Firescrew, named for a terrible fire that occurred there in 1855 and sent up spirals of smoke and fire that could be seen from miles away. Just below the summit of Firescrew, the Mowglis Trail meets the Manning Trail, highlighted by cairns and paint markings. Follow the Manning Trail across flat ledges and down through the woods. You'll see the Duke's Ski Trail off to your left. Stay on the Manning Trail, which descends to a spring and over more ledges before entering the woods again, where it intersects the Holt Trail. Retrace your steps back to the Trailhead and logging road to reach the parking lot.

CENTRAL NEW HAMPSHIRE

Concord: Coach and Eagle Trail (66)

Directions: The walk begins at Eagle Square in downtown Concord. Parking is available in the Eagle Square parking lot.

Best Season: Spring, summer, and fall.

Length: About 2 miles. Allow at least half a day for this walk through historic Concord.

Degree of Difficulty: Easy.

Highlights: History comes to life in this capital city that was home to such statesmen as Daniel Webster and President Franklin Pierce.

This self-guided walking tour of Concord begins at Eagle Square, a public park surrounded by shops and restaurants, which gives the walk part of its name. The other part comes from the fact, perhaps unknown to most visitors, that Concord is the birthplace of the Concord Coach, used for many years by Wells Fargo to carry money, mail, and people westward. The coach was first developed in 1827 by Concord residents Lewis Downing and J. Stephen Abbot. Downing was a wheelwright and Abbot a coach builder.

From Eagle Square, it's an easy walk to the many historic sites in the city, including the New Hampshire State House at 107 N. Main Street. This is the oldest state capital in the United States in which a legislature still meets in its original chambers. The granite building was constructed in 1819 by prison convicts. Inside there are over 150 portraits of major New Hampshire political figures, as well as murals and documents depicting the state's history.

On the grounds of the State House are other sites honoring New Hampshire's history. There are five statues, for example, commemorating New Hampshire statesmen Daniel Webster, John Parker Hale (the first person elected to the Senate on an antislavery platform), Revolutionary War hero John Stark, President Franklin Pierce, and Civil War hero George Hamilton Perkins. Two bronze plaques honor Lafayette's visit to Concord in 1825, and there's a replica of the Liberty Bell (one of fifty-three in the country).

Concord, now a city of close to 35,000 people, began in 1659 as nothing more than an unnamed trading post on the Merrimack River. There's a bend in the river the Indians called *Penny Cook*, and here, in 1697, Hannah Dustin escaped from her Indian captors. She had been kidnapped from her home in Haverhill, Massachusetts.

As the number of settlers to the area increased, land was granted to them, and in 1725, the region was named Plantation of Penacook. In 1733, the name was changed to Rumford, and in 1765, Governor Wentworth changed the name once again, this time to Concord. For an extensive look at the history of the state, visit the New Hampshire Historical Society at 30 Park Street. There, in a building designed in 1911 by Guy Lowell, who also designed the Boston Museum of Fine Arts, you'll find a library of 50,000 volumes, as well as changing exhibits of the history of New Hampshire and of its decorative and fine arts.

SOUTHWESTERN NEW HAMPSHIRE

Mt. Monadnock (67)

Directions: Mt. Monadnock is located in Monadnock State Park, Jaffrey Center, about 80 miles west-northwest of Boston. Take Route 3 north from Boston to Nashua, New Hampshire, and drive west on Route 101A to Route 101. At Peterborough, turn left (south) on Route 202, and continue to Jaffrey. Take Route 124 west from Jaffrey for 2 miles to Dublin Road on the right. Take Dublin Road to Memorial Road, just north of the Monadnock Bible Conference, and turn left. Park Headquarters is on Memorial Road. Leave the pets at home; they are not allowed on Mt. Monadnock.

Best Season: Spring, summer, and fall (during the week, if possible; fall weekends can be crowded).

Length: Trails leading to the summit vary in length from 2 to 4½ miles; average walking time on the most direct route is three or four hours round-trip. There are about 40 miles of trails on the mountain, making this an ideal place for hiking. Allow a full day, if you can.

Degree of Difficulty: Moderately difficult.

Highlights: You'll enjoy beautiful open views from this *monadnock* (an "isolated mountain remnant"), one of the most climbed mountains in America.

Nominator Rebecca Suomala especially likes to walk on Mt. Monadnock for the 360-degree views at the top. "It's the highest mountain in the area," she says, "and you can see into Vermont, Massachusetts, and to the northern parts of New Hampshire. There's not much growing at the summit, so there's nothing to block the views."

There is no question that the 3,165-foot-high Mt. Monadnock (also called Grand Monadnock), which was designated a National Natural Landmark in 1987, is a popular mountain. Since Monadnock and surrounding countryside are probably at their peak beauty in the fall, that's when you'll find the most people. During the last two weekends in September and the first two in October, the park is apt to get filled to capacity and you may be turned away. If you must go at that time, park manager Ben Haubrich suggests you try to get there by 10 a.m. Better yet, hike the mountain during the week, or try visiting it in winter. Cross-country skiing is available, and hiking below the treeline can be wonderful in that season. At times you won't be able to hike to the summit in the winter without ice climbing gear. In fact, you should be conscious of weather conditions whenever you climb Mt. Monadnock. It can be very windy at the summit, and because it is bare rock you are completely exposed to the elements—rain, snow, wind, lightning, etc. Don't take this walk in inclement weather.

Six Trailheads leading to the summit are accessible from roads circling the mountain. All of them are described in an excellent book called *Monadnock Guide*, written by Henry I. Baldwin and published by the Society for the Protection of New Hampshire Forests (SPNHF). The book gives a history of Monadnock, describes its geology and flora and fauna, and gives a variety of valuable and little-known information and advice to make your visit more complete. To get a copy of the book, which costs $8.95, write: Society for the Protection of New Hampshire Forests, 54 Portsmouth Street, Concord, New Hampshire 03301, or call (603) 224-9945. Mt. Monadnock trails are also described in the *White Mountain Guide* of the Appalachian Mountain Club, a handy book for anyone planning a trip to the White Mountains. This book, which costs $13.95, is also available from the SPNHF.

Monadnock State Park Headquarters is a good place to begin any walk on Mt. Monadnock, whether you plan to hike to the summit from here or not (the 1.9-mile White Dot Trail from Park Headquarters is the shortest, most direct route to the top). At the headquarters, rangers can give you up-to-date information on the condition of all the trails, and they can suggest those most suited to your ability, interest, and time. Since there are about 40 miles of trails on the mountain, you have plenty to choose from. There are so many things to see along the various trails that you could easily spend a week or two here and still not see everything, for this mountain has been loved by many people over the years, including Ralph Waldo Emerson (you can visit the Emerson Family Camp Site on the south side of the mountain, just below the summit) and Henry David Thoreau, who identified and collected ninety-four different plant samples during a trip to the mountain in 1860. In a treeless zone near the Pumpelly Trail, you'll find Thoreau Bog, the lowest point in the troughlike fold that forms the top of Monadnock.

The Pumpelly Trail (laid out by Raphael Pumpelly in 1884) is the longest trail to the summit, 4½ miles from Dublin Lake, and it's the one nominator Rebecca Suomala likes best. It starts in the woods, then narrows, and crosses over a stone wall. After about 1 mile, it climbs the steep north end of Pumpelly Ridge and zigzags up to bare rock. A little farther on, you'll come to the Thoreau Bog, and then the Sarcophagus (also called the Boat), a glacial boulder which, from certain angles, resembles a burial sarcophagus, or coffin. From here, watch for the cairns that mark the Pumpelly Trail to the summit. Since the beginning of the Pumpelly Trail is not marked and there is no parking, park officials recommend that you take the Cascade Link, which goes from the park headquarters area to the Pumpelly Trail, near where it breaks out above the trees. By doing this, you can take a different route back to your car.

NORTHERN NEW HAMPSHIRE

The Flume Path and the Pool (68)

Directions: This walk is located in Franconia Notch State Park, in the White Mountain Region of New Hampshire. Exit I-93 (which becomes the Franconia Notch Parkway) at the Flume interchange and follow the Flume access road to the parking area. There is an admission fee: $4 for adults; $2 for children ages 6 to 12.

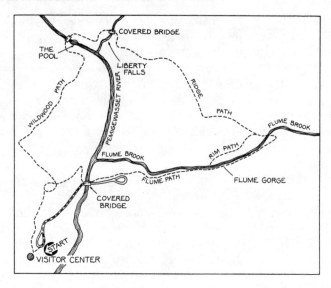

Best Season: Spring and fall; the Flume is open from May 28 to October 23, daily, 9 a.m. to 4:30 p.m.

Length: Just under 2 miles round-trip; allow at least an hour.

Degree of Difficulty: Moderate; the trail is graded and hilly. Stay on the path and behind the rail.

Highlights: This is a unique walk through an 800-foot natural gorge (many think there is nothing quite like it anywhere else on earth), and on to high overlooks above the Pool, a basin in the river which is 40 feet deep and 150 feet in diameter.

The walk begins at the Visitor Center, climbs uphill, and passes by a large boulder weighing some 580 tons, then goes downhill and crosses the Pemigewasset River on a walkway beside one of the more picturesque covered bridges in the state. From this point, it is an uphill climb of more than ¼ mile to and through the Flume Gorge on a graded gravel path, over bridges, and along wooden walkways. Just beyond the gorge, you come to the junction of the Rim Path and the Ridge Path. If you select the Rim Path, you will loop back to the

Flume Path and retrace your steps back to the Visitor Center. The more scenic route is to follow the Ridge Path for ¾ mile downhill to the Pool where the name of the path changes to Wildwood.

Along the Wildwood Path, you will view Liberty Falls and cross the river on a covered bridge, constructed on top of a large pine tree, 16 feet in circumference. For centuries this 175-foot-high tree stood on a cliff above the Pool and was known as the Sentinel Pine. It fell during a hurricane in 1938, and now serves as a base for the covered bridge. After viewing the Pool from cliffs 130 feet high, you climb 200 meters uphill from the river, where there are lovely views of Mt. Flume and Mt. Liberty. From here, continue on for ½ mile, through an area of large boulders, back to the Visitor Center. Nominator Charles Whiton suggests you take the walk early in the morning or late in the afternoon when you'll have the best chance to see wild-life—deer, chipmunks, squirrels, and maybe even a moose or two!

The natural 800-foot chasm known as the Flume was discovered in 1808 by a 93-year-old woman who stumbled upon it while out for a day of fishing. As you take this walk, you will be able to imagine the skepticism that greeted "Aunt" Jess Guernsey when she tried to describe her discovery to her family. But seeing was believing, and while they may not have understood how or why the magnificent gorge came to be, the Guernseys knew it was there.

In fact, forces of nature beginning more than 200 million years ago created the gorge. Fractures broke the granite that forms the walls of the Flume today, and later, basalt from deep within the earth was forced up along the fractures with such pressure that the granite was pushed aside. At that time the granite was underneath the earth's surface, but over the years, erosion lowered this surface and, as waters from the roaring Flume Brook got into the rock layers, the basalt dikes eroded faster than the granite, creating the gorge you see now.

Of course, you really don't have to understand the geologic forces that created the Flume to appreciate its grandeur. Charles Whiton says that from the boardwalk through the chasm, you are not only dwarfed by the 70- to 90-foot-high granite cliffs, you can also peer down at Flume Brook, which glows underneath, making its way through the valley. From this vantage point, you get a good look at the ferns and mosses that grow abundantly on the walls of the al-ways cool, moist gorge.

NORTHERN NEW HAMPSHIRE

Lost River Gorge Walk (69)

Directions: From I-93, take exit 32 at North Woodstock and head west on Route 112 to Kinsman Notch. Lost River is 6 miles west of North Woodstock at the juncture of U.S. 3 and the Kancamagus Highway. There is a $5 admission charge to the gorge and caves for adults; $2.50 for children ages 6 to 12.

Best Season: The gorge is open from mid-May to mid-October. Summer is a good time because there is not as much rain, but it is also the most crowded season.

Length: ¾ mile round-trip. Allow about an hour.

Degree of Difficulty: Moderately difficult; there are a lot of stairs in the gorge, and the entrance trail descends about 300 vertical feet. Benches are provided both on the trail and in the gorge where you can stop to rest. Wear comfortable shoes with rubber or nonslippery soles. Be careful with valuables such as your wallet, sunglasses, camera, and handbag while going through the caves; the river has consumed many of these over the years.

Highlights: This is a unique walk back in time to a natural, untouched world more than 10,000 years old.

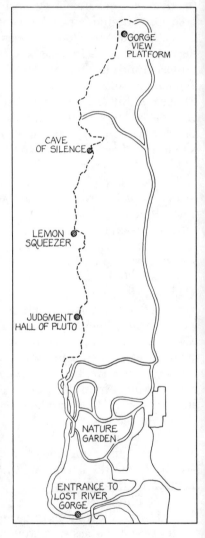

GORGE VIEW PLATFORM

CAVE OF SILENCE

LEMON SQUEEZER

JUDGMENT HALL OF PLUTO

NATURE GARDEN

ENTRANCE TO LOST RIVER GORGE

The Lost River Gorge was formed when glaciers passed over the top of Kinsman Notch more than 10,000 years ago and locked the area in a sheet of moving ice. As the glaciers receded, the melting water raced through the Lost River Valley creating a gorge at least 50 feet deep. Over the years, huge chunks of rock broke off the sides of the gorge to form the caves. Ladders lead down into many of these caves so you can explore them. Some are easy to walk into, but others require a great deal of agility. Pick up a guide before entering the gorge; it provides information about the gorge and describes how to negotiate the various caves and their degree of difficulty. You don't have to enter any of them if you don't want to; they are all side trips off the main trail.

Kim Nolan, who told us about this walk, says that you can hear or see the Lost River in all of the caves but one: the Cave of Silence, which has an eerie quiet to it which you notice right away. One of the most beautiful caves is called the Judgment Hall of Pluto. Here you'll find an underground waterfall which cascades down from a height of 20 feet. At certain times of year, you won't be able to see this, because the water on the floor of the cave gets too deep. The most difficult cave to enter is called The Lemon Squeezer (*to be attempted by only the most agile*). Instructions for negotiating this cave are "harrowingly" specific: "It is best entered head and left shoulder first on your side in a squat position."

Remember, however, that you don't have to visit the caves to enjoy the magnificent beauty of Lost River Gorge. Despite the fact that thousands of people visit this place every year, it has managed to retain a feeling of remoteness and otherworldliness. A variety of plant and animal life thrive in the gorge, including lichens and mosses, ferns, blueberries, and numerous wildflowers. Spruce, fir, and yellow birch trees grow from cracks in the rocks. Animals you may encounter include raccoons, red squirrels, chipmunks, beavers, and, on the larger side, bears and moose.

There are picnic areas at Lost River Gorge, a Nature Garden with more than 300 varieties of native flowers, ferns, and shrubs, and a number of geologic and ecological displays.

NORTHERN NEW HAMPSHIRE

Lake Gloriette Trail (70)

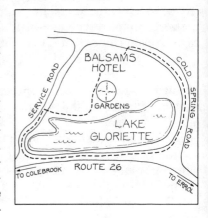

Directions: This walk is located in New Hampshire's White Mountains, at The Balsams Grand Resort Hotel, Dixville Notch, about 219 miles north of Boston. Take I-93 north to exit 35 and drive north on Route 3 to Colebrook. Turn right on Route 26, and continue for approximately 10 miles until you reach Dixville Notch. Lake Gloriette is on the grounds of The Balsams Grand Resort Hotel. From the hotel patio, walk through the gardens, down the steps, and between the tennis courts and pool to the edge of the lake.

Best Season: July 4th through Labor Day.

Length: The walk is a 1.4-mile loop. Allow about three-quarters of an hour.

Degree of Difficulty: Easy.

Highlights: Spectacular vistas in a magnificent wilderness setting high in New Hampshire's White Mountains make this place the "Switzerland of America."

In the summer of 1988, The Balsams, a magnificent 15,000-acre resort hotel, initiated a natural history program which included the development of walking trails throughout the property. In addition to spectacular natural beauty, the area is rich in Indian heritage, and there is good evidence that the region has supported some 12,000 years of human civilization. An archaeologist was hired to oversee the development of the trails, and now, thanks to the generosity and enthusiasm of The Balsams staff, many of these trails are open to the public. If you have the time, explore some of the more remote areas of the property after you have completed the Lake Gloriette Trail, which has long been a favorite of guests at the hotel.

There are directional markers and some explanatory signs relating facts about the ecology and environs on the Lake Gloriette Trail; from the water's edge, bear right along the lake on the Spur Road (the service entrance to Route 26). Turn left, and walk east on the shoulder of the road facing the traffic. At Cold Spring Road, the hotel's main entrance, turn left and loop back to the hotel, where you can enjoy the beautiful formal gardens, composed of some 20,000 plants, or stop for a buffet lunch. (Reservations are suggested for lunch; call (603) 255-3400.)

The Lake Gloriette Trail was nominated by Leonard Reed, who says, "This walk offers spectacular vistas in a magnificent wilderness setting, as well as up-close exposure to a grand variety of wildflowers, cultivated flowers, native trees, and some wildlife." A morning walk is best for seeing birds (the area is one of five nesting sites in the northeast for the peregrine falcon); a sunny afternoon is best to see the butterflies. As you bear right—away from the hotel—at the start of the walk, note the abundance and variety of wildflowers. Many of the plants you see are European imports, wayside plants brought by white settlers from their colonial gardens. Others, such as the tall, golden-yellow Robbin's ragwort, are native to the North Country. The plant was named for its discoverer, James Robbins, a nineteenth-century botanist who also discovered *Potentilla robbinsiana*, a plant with a tiny yellow flower that is listed on the Federal Registry of Endangered Species because it grows in only one place in the entire world (on Mt. Washington). Most of the flowers that grow along Lake Gloriette, unlike *Potentilla robbinsiana*, are fairly common. The wild iris, or blue flag, however, is not; enjoy it on your walk, but don't touch it.

For a longer walk into a more secluded area, you can follow the Reservoir and Canal trails to Mud Pond where you will be surrounded by spruce and balsam fir, the tree which lends its name to the hotel.

NORTHERN NEW HAMPSHIRE

Mt. Washington: Alpine Garden Walk (71)

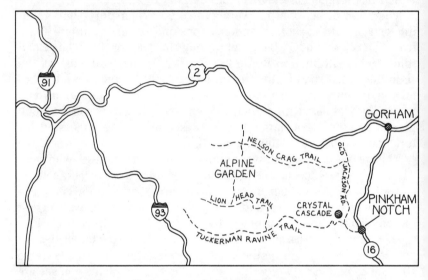

Directions: The walk is located on Mt. Washington and is accessible from Pinkham Notch. Take Route 2 (west from I-95 in Maine, east from I-93 in New Hampshire and I-91 in Vermont) to the town of Gorham where you can pick up Route 16 south to Pinkham Notch. Watch for signs to the Pinkham Notch Trail Center.

Best Season: June.

Length: 7½ to 8 miles. Allow five to six hours.

Degree of Difficulty: Moderately difficult; the elevation is high and the trail is rocky and windy in parts. Wear good hiking shoes.

Highlights: A magnificent alpine garden with many rare plants is the highlight of this walk on Mt. Washington in New Hampshire's White Mountains.

Mt. Washington is the tallest (6,288 feet) mountain in a series of eight peaks in New Hampshire's White Mountains known as the Presidential Peaks, and it is the scene for dramatic extremes in weather conditions. The summit is often blanketed in clouds, and the highest wind velocity ever measured anywhere on land—231 mph—was recorded there in April 1934. The Mt. Washington Observatory, a weather research station at the summit, had to be bolted to the rocks and protected by stone "battlements" in order to withstand the tremendous forces of the wind. There are three ways to reach the summit: on foot, by car or van (guided tours are available from mid-May through October when the road is open), or via a cog railway. Weather permitting, the trip is not to be missed.

Even more than a hike to the summit of Mt. Washington, nominator Alan Lambert likes to walk to the beautiful alpine garden on the mountain, where rare plants bloom profusely for a short time in June. To get there from the Pinkham Notch Trail Center (elevation 2,000 feet), look for the Tuckerman Ravine Trail, a wide path that was originally built for tractors. Follow this trail through the woods and across the Cutler River. Just after you cross the bridge, look for a short side path. This leads to an excellent view of Crystal Cascade, one of the prettiest waterfalls in the White Mountains. Back on the Tuckerman Ravine Trail, you'll find that the trail narrows as you climb to a ridge, which is about 1,200 feet higher than when you started. From here you'll have a magnificent view down into Tuckerman Ravine, a glacial cirque, and out across the mountains over what Alan calls "a lunar landscape." On a clear day you can see for a hundred miles.

From the ravine, follow the trail to its juncture with the Lion Head Trail. The Tuckerman Ravine Trail goes on up to the summit of Mt. Washington, but to see the alpine garden, follow the Lion Head Trail to the top of Lion Head (5,000 feet in elevation). From here, you'll see the Alpine Garden Trail, which leads to a tundra environment covered with beautiful and rare alpine plants. "June is the best month here," Alan says, "for you can experience the full impact of the alpine gardens in bloom then."

From the alpine garden, take the Nelson Crag Trail down to the Old Jackson Road, which leads back to Pinkham Notch.

NORTHERN NEW HAMPSHIRE

A Walk to the Gorham Lead Mines (72)

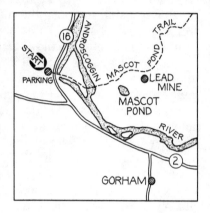

Directions: Gorham is located at the juncture of Routes 2 and 16. Take Route 16 to the north end of town, and park at the B & M Railroad Bridge.

Best Season: Fall, especially the last week of September or the first week of October.

Length: About 1.1 miles. This is a twenty-five or thirty-minute walk.

Degree of Difficulty: Easy to moderate.

Highlights: Beautiful views of the Androscoggin River Valley are the bonus to this fascinating walk through the tunnel of an abandoned lead mine.

From the railroad bridge (known locally as Black Bridge), walk along the footbridge beneath the trestle that crosses the Androscoggin River. Turn right on the dirt road that runs parallel to the river and leads to the powerhouse. In addition to deciduous trees such as birches and maples, you will probably see deer along the path, and nominator Mike Pelchat says you may even spot a moose or a bear!

From the powerhouse, walk up the Mt. Hayes Trail, and continue for about fifteen or twenty minutes, following the blue blazes on the trees along the babbling brook to Mascot Pond at the base of a rocky slope. It's a great scramble over the rocks to the top of this 300-foot slope where you'll be rewarded with a sensational view of the Androscoggin River Valley, the village of Gorham and Mounts Madison, Adams, and Washington (the highest peaks in the northeast). "This is a great place for a picnic!" Mike exclaims. "It's very beautiful, and there are never too many people here."

The mine tunnels on the top of the slope date from the 1800s (the slope itself is a result of debris from the mines). There are two tunnels, an upper and a lower, about 100 feet apart. You can enter the lower one which is level and always nice and cool, but Mike says to avoid the upper one where you may be in danger of walking into an open mine shaft. Another reason to avoid the upper tunnel (at least during the winter) is that bats use it as a home during hibernation. In 1987, wildlife experts counted over 1,000 hibernating bats. "Don't worry about them in the summer, though," Mike says. "There are no bats here then, and even if there were, they are helpful to humans since they consume over ten times their weight in mosquitoes and black flies each night."

Rhode Island

EASTERN RHODE ISLAND

A Stroll through Providence (73)

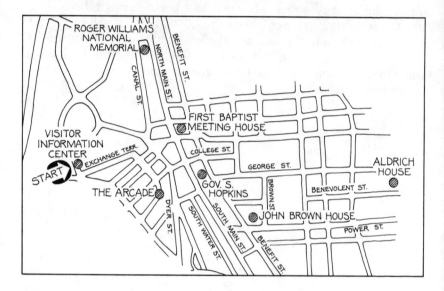

Directions: The walk begins at the Visitor Information Center, 30 Exchange Terrace.

Best Season: Year-round.

Length: Allow at least half a day to explore Providence; more, if you want to spend time in the museums or stop in any of the many shops and restaurants.

Degree of Difficulty: Easy.

Highlights: Benefit Street's "Mile of History," one of America's most beautiful capitol buildings, art galleries, museums, and Brown University are just some of the many things to see in Providence.

The people of Rhode Island are proud of their 300-plus year history, and it shows in their lovely capital city on Narragansett Bay. When you walk down Benefit Street, for example, known as the "Mile of History," you'll be reminded that Providence was also a colonial capital. Benefit Street boasts one of the most impressive collections of original Colonial homes in America. Many of them are open to the public during the Festival of Historic Homes. For more information about these homes, contact the Providence Preservation Society, 21 Meeting Street, Providence, Rhode Island 02903.

Nominator John Flaherty suggests you also visit the John Brown House at 52 Power Street. Built in 1786 for John Brown, who began the China trade in Providence, the house has been carefully restored and contains an extensive collection of Colonial furniture. According to John Flaherty, John Quincy Adams said this house was one of the most elegant he had ever seen. It's open to the public, and there is an admission charge.

At the Roger Williams National Memorial at North Main and Smith streets, you can stand on the site of the original 1636 settlement. Williams came to Providence after having been exiled from the Massachusetts Bay Colony by the Puritans because he had challenged the power of the church and had fought hard for Indian rights. This independent thinking on the part of the founder of Providence has been a hallmark of Rhode Island ever since.

There are several other places of historic interest in Providence, including the Governor Stephen Hopkins House, which was built in 1707 and was the home of Stephen Hopkins, governor of Rhode Island ten times and a signer of the Declaration of Independence. The self-guided walking tour brochure of Providence exclaims: "George Washington slept here twice!" The Museum of Rhode Island History at Aldrich House provides more information and changing exhibits on Rhode Island's history. History enthusiasts will not want to miss the First Baptist Meeting House at 75 North Main Street. The congregation of the First Baptist Church in America was founded in 1638 by Williams and his followers. This meeting house was built in 1775 and has been restored to retain its original beauty. Still used as a church, the meeting house is also the site for Brown University's commencement ceremonies.

John particularly recommends that you visit Brown while you're in Providence. Founded in 1764, it's the seventh oldest university in the United States. University Hall was used as a barracks and hospital during the revolution.

At some point during your walk, take a break at the Arcade, a National Historic Landmark and the oldest indoor shopping center in America. The beautiful old building provides an elegant setting for shopping, eating, or simply strolling around. And John suggests you visit Federal Hill, Providence's "Little Italy," where wonderful Italian restaurants and sidewalk cafés, and even a piazza with its own fountain make you feel a little bit as if you were in Rome!

EASTERN RHODE ISLAND

Lincoln Woods (74)

Directions: Lincoln Woods Park is in eastern Rhode Island, not too far from Providence. Take I-95 to Route 146, and exit at Lincoln Woods. Entrance to the park is via Twin Rivers Road.

Best Season: Spring through fall. There is a nominal admission fee from Memorial Day to Labor Day; at other times entrance is free.

Length: This walk is a 2½-mile loop.

Degree of Difficulty: Easy.

Highlights: This is a country walk around a lovely pond that is easy to get to and fairly close to major towns and cities.

This easy walk through the woods and around Olney Pond is a wonderful getaway spot as well as a terrific place to take the kids for a Sunday outing. Olney Pond is particularly picturesque, with its coves and wooded islands, and it affords something for everybody: swimming, boating, fishing, strolling. Bring a picnic lunch with you so you can take full advantage of this lovely place.

The walk around the pond leads past an old cemetery where nominator Dennis Doire says members of the Olney family, for whom the pond was named, are buried. Some of the tombstones date back to the eighteenth century. The cemetery may be a good place to reflect on Rhode Island's early and continuing contribution to America's basic tenet—freedom. Since 1636, when Roger Williams—exiled by the Puritans in Massachusetts—founded Providence, Rhode Island has been a vocal defender of freedom and has provided a haven for the persecuted. It may be the smallest state, but when push comes to shove, there is no doubt it won't be the quietest.

SOUTHEASTERN RHODE ISLAND

Colt Park and Prudence Island (75)

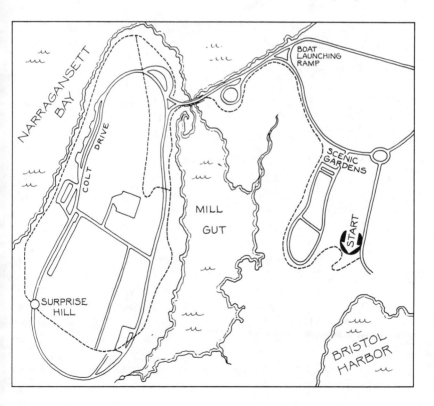

Directions: The walk begins at Colt Park on the north end of Bristol, Rhode Island, off Route 114 on Hope Street. The entrance is marked by two stone gateposts with a bull on top of each one. From Colt Park, drive into Bristol to Thames Street where you can take the Homestead Ferry to Prudence Island. Call the Prudence Island Navigation Company (401) 253-9808 for schedule information.

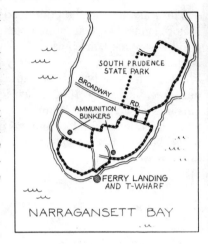

Best Season: Spring through fall; ferry service is best in the summer months.

Length: About 3 miles in Colt Park; about 8 miles on Prudence Island. Allow a full day.

Degree of Difficulty: Easy.

Highlights: Wonderful views of the bay combine with wildlife and birds on the scenic walk on Prudence Island; Colt Park gives you an initial taste for the lovely Narragansett Bay.

This walk, nominated by Kevin O'Malley, is really two walks in one. It starts in Colt Park where you can spend some time exploring the salt marshes and beaches of Narragansett Bay. Then, get in your car and drive into Bristol to pick up the Homestead Ferry for Prudence Island.

From the ferry landing in the village of Homestead, walk to South Prudence State Park, where you can explore this peaceful island, not yet spoiled by too many homes or visitors. Kevin says most of the homes you see are summer homes only. In addition to spectacular views of the bay, you'll pass by some old military bunkers (in World War II, the island was a key point in the defense plans for Narragansett Bay) and some vineyards with hundreds of rows of grapevines. A nature trail begins at the T-Wharf where you can pick up a self-guided trail brochure that explains points of significance along the way.

There is a bird sanctuary on the north end of the island, but it's a long walk from the Homestead ferry landing to the north end. There are plans to increase service on the north-end ferry, but at present it is not running on a regular basis. You'll see plenty of birds on this walk through the southern end of the island, though—cormorants, gulls, terns, and other water birds, as well as a variety of other birds who love to eat the berries that grow on the many bushes and vines on the island. And there are lots of deer on Prudence Island; in fact, the island has the densest deer population in New England.

SOUTHEASTERN RHODE ISLAND

Ruecker Wildlife Refuge (76)

Directions: The refuge is located just south of Tiverton, Rhode Island. From Fall River, Massachusetts, take Route 24 south through Tiverton to Route 138. Make a left off 138 to Route 77, then turn right on Sapowet Avenue. The refuge is ¼ mile down Sapowet on your right.

Best Season: Spring through fall.

Length: Only about 1½ miles, but this is a fascinating place, so leave lots of time to enjoy it.

Degree of Difficulty: Easy.

Highlights: Hundreds of birds, shallow marshes, and beautiful woodlands create a perfect place to walk and enjoy nature.

Trails marked in yellow, red, and blue wind through this beautiful wildlife refuge, which was once a 50-acre farm. In 1965, Emilie Ruecker donated it to the Audubon Society of Rhode Island, which has, through careful management, made it a thriving sanctuary for birds. As many as 150 different species visit the refuge during the year. In the fall, migrating swallows stop here before continuing their journey south; in both spring and fall, you'll see herons, bitterns, sandpipers, and a variety of ducks; in winter, a bird feeding station stocked by the Audubon Society attracts numerous birds, including chickadees and nuthatches. Nominator Al Hawkes advises that the best place to observe heron is at the salt marsh adjacent to the refuge. The marsh is also a good place to see a number of different shorebirds, including the big egrets.

Along the beach, you can watch the fascinating fiddler crabs, named for their one large claw that someone once thought looked like a big fiddle. In the summer you'll find them scrambling along the sand or hiding in the tiny holes you see just about everywhere.

If you follow the red trail, you'll come to rock ledges estimated to be some 250 million years old. They are composed of small pebbles which look as if they have been cemented together; this type of rock is called *pudding stone*.

After your walk through the refuge, you may want to visit the Green Animals Topiary Gardens off Route 114 in Portsmouth. Located on Cory's Lane, the gardens include some of the finest examples of animal topiary in the country. You'll see all kinds of animals— a giraffe, an elephant, a lion, a tiger—as well as tall towers, spirals, baskets, arches, and other formations. The gardens are open daily from May 1 to September 30 and on weekends in October.

SOUTHEASTERN RHODE ISLAND

Fort Adams (77)

Directions: The fort is located in Newport, Rhode Island. From points south, take I-95 north to Route 138 east. Cross the Newport Bridge and turn right. From points north, head for Route 114 south, which leads into Newport.

Best Season: Spring, summer, and fall.

Length: ½ mile perimeter. Allow about two hours for your "inspection" of Fort Adams.

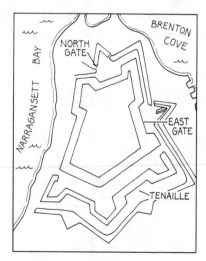

Degree of Difficulty: Easy.

Highlights: An up-close look at America's military history from the 1820s to the end of World War II.

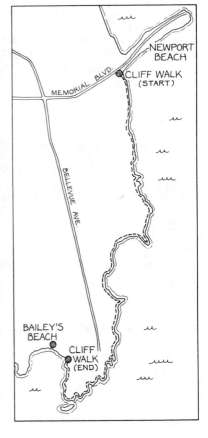

This walk around Fort Adams, one of the largest seacoast fortifications in the United States, is a fascinating military history lesson. The fort was dedicated in 1799 when John Adams, America's second president, was in office. An inscription over the entrance arch once read: "Fort Adams, the Rock on which the Storm will beat." Initially, it was not a terribly solid rock and by 1812, the fort was in disrepair. The burning of Washington during the War of 1812 convinced the government that America needed to improve its coastal defenses. Work began to reconstruct Fort Adams in 1824 and was not completed until 1857. The total cost was $3 million.

Conceived along the lines of fortification design developed by the Marquis de Vauban, military engineer to France's King Louis XIV, the fort contains an earth-and-masonry structure known as the Tenaille. It was designed to protect the main fort from cannon fire and is found nowhere else in the United States. The fact that Fort Adams never was attacked is probably a tribute to the strength of its fortification design, which included three tiers of cannon to protect against attacks from the sea and extensive earthworks to protect against land assault.

Fort Adams was originally intended to protect the entrance to Narragansett Bay, but it became the command center for the complex of coastal batteries in the northeast that protected both the Narragansett Bay and Long Island Sound through the end of World War II.

Following your walk around the fort, plan to take Newport's renowned Cliff Walk. This 3-mile National Recreation Trail begins at Memorial Boulevard and follows the coast to Bailey's Beach. The views from the trail are spectacular, with water vistas on one side and some of America's most magnificent mansions on the other.

NORTHERN RHODE ISLAND
Parker Woodland (78)

Directions: From I-95, take Route 102 north, and turn east on Maple Valley Road. Stop in at the first house on your left, which is Parker Woodland Headquarters, for a self-guided pamphlet that describes numerous points of interest along the trails. The parking lot is about ¼ mile farther down on Maple Valley Road.

Best Season: Spring and fall.

Length: About 7 or 8 miles, but there are several alternative routes, and you can turn back any time if you don't want to hike the full distance.

Degree of Difficulty: Moderately difficult; the trail goes up and down in parts.

Highlights: In addition to beautiful woods and scenery, this walk captures a part of Rhode Island's past.

In 1983, a team of archaeologists from Brown University explored an old homesite located near the start of this trail through Parker Woodland. Signs describing what they found give you some insight into what life was like in this area in the 1700s. Farther along the trail, you'll come to other archaeological sites: two charcoal processing plants and a once-thriving farm. It's a little difficult to imagine, perhaps, that this peaceful setting was once considered a "dangerous" area. Apparently taverns along Maple Valley Road attracted some

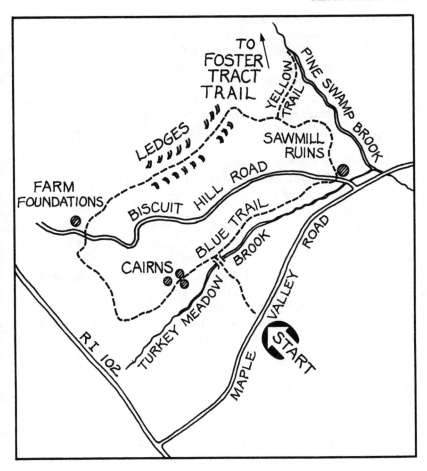

pretty rough characters, and the tales of fighting and shooting are too common to be disregarded.

Your walk through Parker Woodland will take you by dozens of stone *cairns,* pyramid-shaped structures that are still a puzzle to archaeologists, sociologists, and others who have tried to determine their origin. To date, no one has satisfactorily explained what these cairns are or even exactly how old they are. You can examine them up close, but don't touch them; the Audubon Society of Rhode Island, which manages Parker Woodland, does not want them disturbed.

There are numerous other places of interest in Parker Woodland, including an old sawmill, which nominator Al Hawkes says dates from the Civil War. The sawmill is located off a dirt road called Biscuit Hill Road. The name is supposed to have derived from a Revolutionary War incident. In 1780, Count Rochambeau landed at Newport with an army of 6,000 men, ready to help George Washington fight the British. Apparently, a wagon load of biscuits on its way to Rochambeau and his men was spilled here. Memory of the incident is preserved in the name of the road—Biscuit Hill.

As you walk through Parker Woodland, you'll come to the picturesque Pine Swamp Brook, filled with a number of waterfalls and pools. It's a nice place to sit and imagine yourself back two or three hundred years.

From Pine Swamp Brook, follow the yellow-blazed trail to its intersection with the Foster Tract Trail, which is marked in blue. You can turn back here, if you want, and return to your car, or you can follow the blue-blazed trail farther into the woods. If you decide to continue, you'll pass some old stone foundations, a cellar hole to an old farmhouse, an old well, and, seemingly in the middle of nowhere, a stone fireplace. Stone walls stop and start along the way, probably marking some ancient boundary, or maybe they were just put there long ago when someone was clearing the fields.

Eventually, the blue trail connects again with the yellow trail, which leads back to your car.

SOUTHERN RHODE ISLAND

Rodman's Hollow (79)

Directions: Rodman's Hollow Preserve is located in the southwest corner of Block Island. Ferries leave for the island from Point Judith year-round (the trip takes about an hour and a quarter) and from Providence during the summer (a four-hour trip). Once on the island, take Center Road to Cooneymus Road (which becomes West Side Road). Drive 0.8 mile west, and turn left on Black Rock Road. Follow the road to the parking lot in the center of the preserve.

Best Season: Spring, summer, and fall.

Length: There are a number of old trails that wind through the hollows and hills. Plan on spending at least half a day here.

Degree of Difficulty: Easy.

Highlights: A wonderful opportunity to observe hawks, migratory birds, and the ocean.

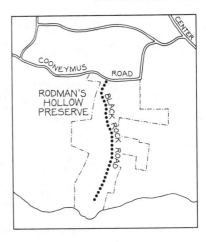

Block Island lies about 10 miles off the southern coast of Rhode Island and despite its popularity with summer visitors, it remains relatively unspoiled. A 3-mile route along the southeast coast from where the ferry docks to Mohegan Bluffs makes a nice walk, with wonderful views. The bluffs are composed of sand and boulders, left behind when the glaciers melted.

One of the best places, however, to view Block Island in its pristine state is at the Rodman's Hollow Preserve. (If you decide to take the 3-mile walk from the ferry to Mohegan Bluffs, you may want to continue on Lakeside Drive for about another 6 miles or so to the preserve.) Block Island has always been a special place because it provides a resting and feeding habitat for migrant birds. Now approximately 200 acres have been preserved at Rodman's Hollow. Here, and at the adjacent Lewis-Dickens Farm, is the largest concentration of rare bird, plant, and invertebrate species on the island.

Rodman's Hollow not only provides extensive feeding grounds for the endangered northern harrier or marsh hawk, its remnant grassy openings provide habitat for rare plants. Be sure to stay on the trails that wind through the hollows and hills so that you don't disturb anything in this delicately balanced area. Guided walks are sponsored by the state Department of Environmental Management (DEM). For more information, write the DEM, 22 Hayes Street, Providence, RI 02908, or call (401) 277-2771. In addition to walking in the preserve, you can surf-cast at Black Rock Point.

SOUTHWESTERN RHODE ISLAND

Tippecansett Trail (80)

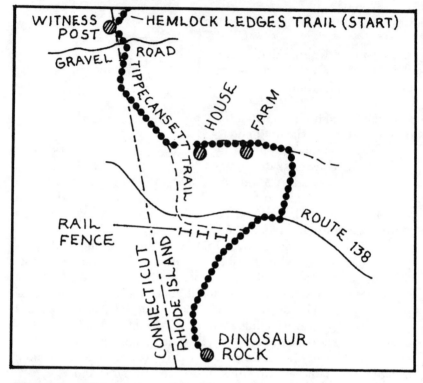

Directions: This section of the Tippecansett Trail starts in western Rhode Island, in the village of Rockville. Take exit 3 off I-95, and head northwest on Route 138 to Rockville. You can park in the parking area in the village.

Best Season: Year-round; but spring is particularly beautiful when the mountain laurel are in bloom.

Length: This segment is 7¼ miles. The entire Tippecansett Trail is 45½ miles long and intersects numerous other trails, including some that begin in Connecticut.

Degree of Difficulty: Moderately difficult; there are some inclines.

Highlights: A peaceful walk through a diversity of landscapes, including pine and hemlock forests and woods of mountain laurel and rhododron.

Tippecansett is the longest trail in Rhode Island; if you can't walk all of it, nominator Tom Armstrong recommends this 7¼-mile segment because it offers a wide variety of terrain.

There is an incline at the beginning of the yellow-blazed trail which leads over a wooden bridge and on up to the edge of a deep ravine. As you continue along the sandy road, you'll be on the Connecticut border; look for a stone marker with "C" chiseled on one side and "RI" on the other. You'll see a lot of wildlife here or at least evidence of it. Look for deer tracks, and listen for grouse rustling in the bushes.

Continue following the yellow blazes, which mark the Tippecansett Trail. When you reach the gravel road, you are on the Hemlock Ledges segment of the trail. Take this trail to the Witness Post, which is a state boundary marker, then return to the Tippecansett Trail and retrace your steps. Just over the wooden bridge you crossed earlier, there is a cutoff trail on your left. This leads through dense forests and climbs to a slight opening where you can see the remains of an old house: the foundation, remnants of a huge fireplace, and an old well and cellar hole. The artistry of these old stoneworks is impressive.

Beyond this spot, the trail narrows, then opens up again and follows fences and stone walls to some farm buildings. From here, walk along the roadway, and turn right at the first fork. This will lead you back to Route 138. Turn right and watch for a lane entering the woods on your left. This picturesque pathway, lined with stone walls, rejoins the yellow-blazed Tippecansett Trail. Walk left on the trail, and continue to Dinosaur Rock, a smooth ledge which affords an impressive view. Spend as much time as you like here, savoring the tranquility and beauty of the place.

When you're ready to return, retrace your steps to where the yellow blazes reappear. Turn left and follow the old rail fence back to Route 138.

SOUTHWESTERN RHODE ISLAND

Ben Utter Trail (81)

Directions: From Route 3, take Route 165 west for about 3 miles to Frosty Hollow Road on your right. Continue to the end of this gravel lane (about 1½ miles), and turn left. After about 2 miles, turn left again and park on your right, just beyond the bridge.

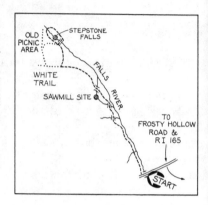

Best Season: Year-round; each season offers something unique.

Length: 3½ miles round-trip.

Degree of Difficulty: Moderately difficult.

Highlights: You'll pass by remnants of an old gristmill and sawmill, and walk through beautiful forest areas on your way to the main attraction: magnificent Stepstone Falls.

This is a short, relaxing, and picturesque trail, which Tom Armstrong nominated because it leads to the wonderful Stepstone Falls. The trail is marked with yellow blazes, and while you won't be able to see the river all the way, you will be able to hear its rumblings. Near the start, you'll climb up a stone stairway to the remnants of an old gristmill. You can see the foundations on either side of the stream. From here, you'll follow the trail through a thicket of mountain laurel and over a wooden bridge. The stone slabs on your left are all that remain of a vertical sawmill once powered by a waterwheel.

To reach Stepstone Falls, follow the Ben Utter Trail until you see a white-blazed spur trail on your right. After about ½ mile of difficult terrain, you'll be at the falls. Here you can watch the river cascade happily over natural steps from one level to another; it's absolutely beautiful and mesmerizing at the same time. You won't want to leave.

When you must leave, follow the white-blazed trail over the

wooden bridge and around the falls. After completing the circle, look for the stone steps that lead up from the footbridge. The steps will take you to a backpacker's camping area where you can pick up the yellow-blazed Ben Utter Trail again and return to your car.

SOUTHWESTERN RHODE ISLAND

John B. Hudson Trail (82)

Directions: Take Route 165 from Route 3, and drive 2.6 miles west. A small sign on a tree marks the start of the trail. Follow the narrow lane a short way to a parking area on your right.

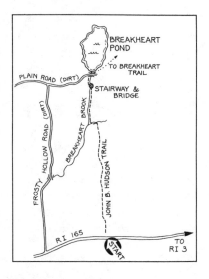

Best Season: Late spring and winter.

Length: 3 miles round-trip.

Degree of Difficulty: Easy, except you may get your feet wet in a few places if you take the walk in early spring.

Highlights: An observation tower along this trail affords an unspoiled panoramic view of nature at its best.

John Hudson was an early "pioneer" hiker in Rhode Island, and this trail, named for him, is one of the oldest in the state. It is also one of the most popular. People love to walk it at all times of the year and to listen and watch for seasonal changes. Late spring is an especially good time to come, for the mountain laurel bloom then; but winter is the most peaceful, and in some ways the most beautiful—there is nothing quite so breathtaking as streams gurgling over packs of ice and snow, under a canopy of crystallike branches. All year the music of songbirds can be heard.

Toward the beginning of the trail, a white-blazed side trail leads to a wooden tower with steps to the top. From here you can see for miles and miles—and it's all beautifully unspoiled, remaining just as the first settlers must have seen it hundreds of years ago.

Follow the trail to a small cemetery, nestled among the pines; some of the stone markers are still legible. Continue on the yellow-blazed trail, along the edge of a brook. Here's where you might get your feet wet if it's early spring. Watch your footing as you cross over the stream on steps of rocks. When you get to higher ground, you'll see a wooden stairway which leads down a steep slope. The stairs were built in 1980 by a youth group and make the walk down a lot easier. The trail now links up with Breakheart Trail (see below), just beyond the picnic area near Breakheart Pond. If you wish, you can take the 1½-mile walk around the pond before heading back to your car the way you came.

SOUTHWESTERN RHODE ISLAND

Breakheart Trail (83)

Directions: Located in Arcadia Management Area, the trail can be reached by taking Route 165 from Route 3. Drive 3 miles west on 165, and turn right at the church on Frosty Hollow Road. Continue to the end of Frosty Hollow, and turn right to Breakheart Pond. The walk begins at the bridge below Fish Ladder Dam.

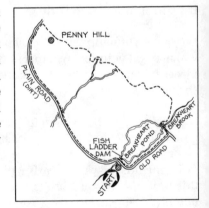

Best Season: Year-round.

Length: 10 miles round-trip.

Degree of Difficulty: Moderately difficult; there is some rocky terrain.

Highlights: A picturesque walk around Breakheart Pond and up through the forest to a panoramic view from Penny Hill.

The name Breakheart Pond, which has a decidedly romantic ring to it, comes not from some legend of a broken heart; it stems from nearby Breakheart Hill, so-named because it was such a heartbreaking job to drive oxen up its slopes.

Fish Ladder Dam, where this walk begins, is a "ladder" for fish or, more accurately, a series of shallow pools that were built to help trout get over the dam so they could return upstream to spawn.

From Fish Ladder Dam, walk to the far end of the pond and follow the yellow-blazed Breakheart Trail over Breakheart Brook and on into the forest. You'll climb past pines and oaks, cross various lanes and gravel roads, and ford a couple of streams before reaching Penny Hill. Keep an eye out for wildlife: A few squirrels and chipmunks will probably join you on your walk. The white signs you see on the trees mark an agricultural and biological research area belonging to the University of Rhode Island.

Penny Hill is 370 feet above sea level, which may not seem very high, but it's the highest point around, and it affords a wonderful view of the forests and surrounding countryside.

After you've enjoyed the vista for a while, head down the opposite side of Penny Hill, and turn left when you reach the gravel road; this leads back to Breakheart Pond.

NORTHEASTERN RHODE ISLAND

Diamond Hill Trail (84)

Directions: The trail is located in Diamond Hill State Park, in the town of Cumberland, in the northeast corner of Rhode Island. From I-295, take a left on Route 114 (Diamond Hill Road), and follow signs to the park.

Best Season: Any nice day in spring, summer, or fall.

Length: About 3 miles. Allow two hours or more.

Degree of Difficulty: Difficult; there's a steep climb up a cliff to the top of Diamond Hill.

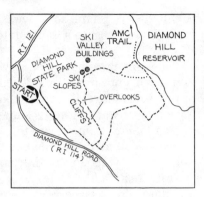

Highlights: From the 150-foot summit of Diamond Hill, there are wonderful views of the village below and the surrounding countryside.

The most exciting part of this walk, nominated by Dennis Doire, is a strenuous but short scramble up Diamond Hill cliff. The beautiful part is at the top. There are actually several worn pathways to the summit, and you can choose just about any one of them. This area used to be popular for skiing, and the concrete foundations at the top of the cliff were once part of a ski lift. The faded yellow marks you may note on various trees and rocks are markers for the Appalachian Mountain Club's Warner Trail, which crosses Diamond Hill and runs all the way to Canton, Massachusetts, just south of Boston.

Spend some time on the high ridge of Diamond Hill, enjoying the views of the village below, the beautiful countryside to the west, and the reservoir. Walking north along the ridge, you'll find that it ends at several gravel lanes. If you take the left one, you'll have a fairly easy downhill walk through the park and back to your car. If you want more of a challenge, keep an eye on the reservoir as your final goal and make your way down the old ski slopes. If you can find any of the yellow AMC markers, follow them, otherwise, use your own instincts.

From the reservoir, you can head back the way you came, or if you feel adventurous, use your own sense of direction to take an alternate route.

If you want to pack a picnic lunch, Dennis says there is a picnic area in Diamond Hill Park, as well as a small pond where you can fish.

CENTRAL VERMONT

Main Street, Poultney Village (85)

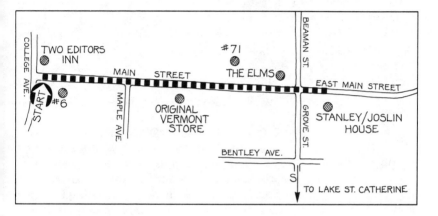

Directions: Poultney is located on the border of New York and Vermont. From Rutland, take Route 4 to Route 30, and head south to Poultney. The walk begins at No. 1 Main Street at the Two Editors Inn.

Best Season: Year-round; each season has its own charm.

Length: Only about 1 mile, but allow about half a day because there's lots to see.

Degree of Difficulty: Easy.

Highlights: In addition to a quaint shopping area, Poultney's wide and charming Main Street is lined with buildings of architectural beauty and diversity.

Poultney was chartered in 1761, although it didn't have any settlers until ten years later, and then there were only two of them. As more people began to arrive, they settled around the Green in what is now East Poultney. Then, in the mid-1800s, when the D & H Railroad came through the "West Village," many people moved to what is now Poultney. The new village became a thriving industrial town with grist mills, a candlestick factory, furniture factories, and even an organ factory. In addition, there were many, many stills! Unfortunately, this industrial activity rose up along the river, and most of it was destroyed by a disastrous flood in 1811. Many people turned to farming until 1850, when a new industry was born out of slate. You will notice that many of the homes in Poultney have slate roofs. Back in the 1800s, workmen came to Poultney to work in the slate business from as far away as the slate quarries of Wales. Interestingly, slate—whether from Wales, Vermont, Pennsylvania, or elsewhere—originated some 450 million years ago as mud on the floor of what was to become known as the Atlantic Ocean.

Today Poultney is a quiet, contented village with a population just over 3,000. This walk along Main Street, which was nominated by Patricia Endlich, provides an opportunity to see wonderful architectural diversity and to learn something about Poultney's history from the people who once lived and worked here. We have highlighted just a few of the buildings; there are many more that you will want to explore for yourself.

The Two Editors Inn, where the walk begins, is named in honor of two Poultney editors, Horace Greeley, who founded the *New York Herald Tribune*, and George Jones, a cofounder of *The New York Times*. Today the inn serves as a guest house for Green Mountain College.

At No. 6 Main Street, you'll find a house from an early Victorian period that was once the home of Col. Judson A. Lewis, a Civil War hero and the U.S. consul to Africa. Mrs. Lewis, who survived her husband by a number of years, must have been quite a character. For example, she is reported to have dressed for the entire week by donning seven dresses on Sunday and removing one each day!

At No. 58 Main is the Original Vermont Store. This Greek Revival house was built around 1840 and was owned at one point by the Sherman family. Mr. Sherman operated a feed and grain business in the mill to the rear, and Mrs. Sherman had a photographic studio next door which she reached via a tunnel under the drive.

The Queen Anne–style building with Italianate and Colonial Revival detailing at 71 Main Street was once a schoolhouse. Today it serves as apartments for senior citizens. The Elms, at 83 Main Street, was built as a hotel and served as a stage stop before belonging to the Beaman family, who lived in the house for over 100 years. Today it is a community care center.

The Stanley/Joslin House at 6 E. Main Street is thought to be one of the oldest homes in Poultney, dating from the first quarter of the nineteenth century. It was built for Henry Stanley, founder of the Stanley Foundry, and it later became the home of Joseph Joslin, a blacksmith, church deacon, and the author of the *History of Poultney*, 1875.

After your walk down Main Street, Patricia Endlich suggests you try a different type of walk by strolling leisurely around beautiful Lake St. Catherine. You can start this walk either at Lake St. Catherine State Park, where there is good swimming, fishing, and picnicking, in season, or at the Lake St. Catherine Inn, on the shores of the lake, south of Poultney on Route 30 (for reservations or information about the inn, call (802) 287-9347). The lake is 7 miles long and, Patricia says, "the cottages along its shoreline are old and offer insight into a quieter, more relaxing time when the great American dream was time spent at a Vermont lakeside resort."

CENTRAL VERMONT

Texas Falls (86)

Directions: From Montpelier, take Route 89 to Route 100B south to Route 100. Continue south on 100 to the town of Hancock. Turn right on Route 125 in Hancock, and look for the Texas Falls Recreation Area, about 3.2 miles west of Hancock on your right. From Rutland, take Route 4 east through Sherburne Pass to Route 100 north. Follow Route 100 north to Hancock, and turn left onto Route 125 to the Texas Falls Recreation Area.

Best Season: Summer and early fall.

Length: There are two nature trails at Texas Falls; the upper trail is ¾ mile, the lower trail is ⅓ mile. You can combine the two to make a loop trail which takes about one and a quarter hours to complete.

Degree of Difficulty: Easy.

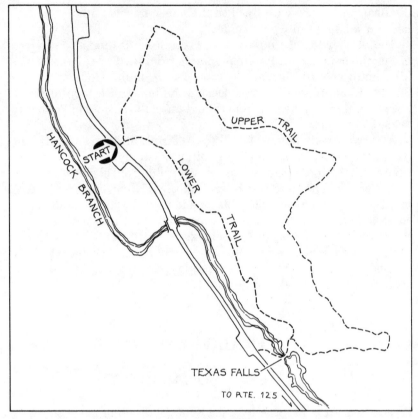

Highlights: A scenic natural waterfall, one of the most beautiful in Vermont, is the highlight of this area.

Texas Falls is a favorite spot of nominator Berniece Kapitan, who says the area is "definitely worth a visit." The waterfall is one of the most beautiful in Vermont, and you will probably want to spend some time watching the water as it cascades down the rocky gorge and catches beams of sunlight, giving it an almost metallic, gemlike quality.

An excellent interpretive trail guide provides fascinating information about the plant and animal life you will encounter on the loop trail. Stay on the trail to avoid damaging any part of this beautiful area. You will see evidence of erosion that has been caused mainly by people walking off the path and compacting the soil with their shoes or boots. Plants cannot grow up through the hard dirt, and without plants there is nothing to hold the soil during hard rains. The result is erosion.

At numerous stations along the trail, the guide explains or describes what you are seeing or hearing. You'll pass through an evergreen forest and by an old large-toothed aspen. You'll see lichens growing on rock, and you'll be able to observe how they influence other plants such as the mosses and ferns that grow nearby. You'll learn about lenticels (vents in the bark of some trees which allow for an exchange of gases between the tissues of the tree and the air), and you'll discover how to recognize the handiwork of the yellow-bellied sapsucker and to appreciate the service this little woodpecker provides to other members of the forest.

When you start the upper trail, you'll be on an old logging road, now reserved for hikers (and snowmobilers in the winter). Along this trail, which follows the side of a ridge, you'll see club mosses, ferns, and a variety of trees and shrubs. The guide will help you to recognize a "deer yard," where the deer gather during the winter and to identify the large rectangular holes made by the pileated woodpecker, the largest woodpecker in Vermont.

Don't forget to plan on spending some time at the spectacular Texas Falls. Bring a picnic lunch and enjoy this beautiful spot for as long as you can.

CENTRAL VERMONT

Robert Frost Trail (87)

Directions: The trail is located in the northern part of the Green Mountain National Forest, east of the town of Ripton, off Route 125 (the Robert Frost Memorial Drive).

Best Season: Summer and fall.

Length: About ½ mile. Allow at least three-quarters of an hour to absorb the beauty and tranquility of the place (and to read the poems).

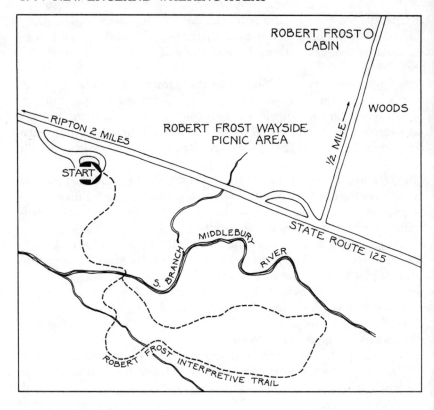

Degree of Difficulty: Easy.

Highlights: A chance to contemplate the words of Robert Frost in a place which inspired them.

> *I shall be telling this with a sigh*
> *Somewhere ages and ages hence:*
> *Two roads diverged in a wood, and I—*
> *I took the one less traveled by,*
> *And that has made all the difference.*

This inspiring walk is just as you might imagine it if you are familiar with the poems of Robert Frost. The trail leads through the woods and fields described so eloquently, yet simply, by this popular American poet who was awarded the Pulitzer Prize for poetry in 1924, 1931, 1937, and 1943, and who came to this area during the summers until his death in 1963.

The walk received two nominations, one from Les Noble, who lives in nearby Middlebury, and one from Penny Phillips, who discovered it while she was taking summer courses at the Middlebury College Language School. Penny's mother is an avid reader of Frost, and so Penny particularly enjoyed discovering the poems placed on posts along the trail. "Everyone in my family says, 'Two roads diverged in a wood...' at every fork in every path," she says, "so you can imagine that, for me, finding those words on a signpost in a wood seemed just like the way nature meant for a path to be. And, of course, the scenery is beautiful. It's Vermont."

After your walk, take Route 125 west to Middlebury College. The road itself is a beautiful one, winding through a forest and following the course of the Middlebury River. Middlebury's parklike campus includes a stately old church which was built between 1806 and 1809. With its 136-foot tower and Palladian window, it is a wonderful example of New England church architecture. Stop in at the Sheldon Museum where you'll find a collection of curios from life in early Vermont and at the Vermont State Craft Center at Frog Hollow where local craftspeople display and sell their work.

CENTRAL VERMONT

Lincoln Gap to Appalachian Gap: A Sampling of the Long Trail (88)

Directions: From Montpelier, take I-89 to Route 100B south, and drive about 18 miles to the town of Warren. From Warren, head west on the Lincoln-Warren Highway, and watch for signs to the Long Trail north, in Lincoln Gap.

Best Season: Late spring through fall.

Length: 11 miles one way; allow three and a half to four hours. You'll need a full day if you plan to hike back as well.

Degree of Difficulty: Moderately difficult; the elevation is high, and this is mountain hiking, not strolling. The terrain can be rocky; wear good hiking boots.

Highlights: There are wonderful views on this hike in the Green Mountains, which begins at an elevation of 2,400 feet.

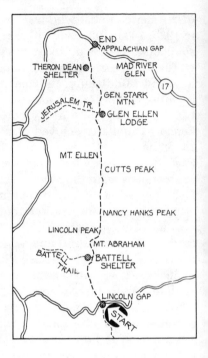

The Long Trail, which stretches some 265 miles from North Troy near the Canadian border to Blackinton, Massachusetts, is Vermont's major hiking trail. Conceived in 1910 by members of the newly formed Green Mountain Club, the trail was completed in 1931, providing, along with numerous side trails, a means for people to walk over the major peaks of the Green Mountains the entire length of the state.

Nominator Mark Aiken likes to recommend the section of the Long Trail from Lincoln Gap to Appalachian Gap as a sampler to visitors because it offers wonderful views and you can drive to an elevation of about 2,400 feet before even starting to walk. "From there you can climb even higher," Mark explains, "and within a few miles you have a spectacular 360-degree view. On a clear day, you can see the White Mountains to the east and Lake Champlain to the west."

From Lincoln Gap, the trail crosses over a knoll and then rises gradually to reach an old mountain road. You will see the Battell Trail junction on your left and the Battell Shelter on your right. Joseph Battell owned an inn west of Middlebury Gap. In 1901, he cut a trail to Mt. Ellen, probably the first skyline trail in the Green Mountains. From the Battell Trail junction, continue north along the white-blazed Long Trail to the summit of Mount Abraham. From this 4,000-foot-plus elevation, you'll enjoy a panoramic view: New Hampshire's

White Mountains are to the east, the Adirondacks to the west, and the Green Mountains stretch out to the north and south. You are above the timberline here, and it is important to stay on the marked trail; plant life in this area is very fragile and can be irrevocably damaged by your hiking boots.

From the Mount Abraham summit, the trail descends and crosses the summits of Little Abe and Lincoln Peak. The large clearing you see is the former site of the Sugarbush Valley Gondola Station. From the clearing, the Long Trail bears left, enters the woods, and heads north again, following the ridge of Lincoln Mountain over Nancy Hanks Peak. At the Castle Rock Chair Lift, the trail descends to Holt Hollow, then climbs to Cutts Peak, and reaches the summit of Mt. Ellen, at 4,083 feet (tied with Camel's Hump as the third-highest mountain in Vermont). From the upper station of the Glen Ellen Chair Lift, just beyond the summit, there are good views to the east and north.

Cross the Mt. Ellen summit, and follow a ski trail for about 100 feet before entering the woods. Now the Long Trail descends and winds along the ridge to the Jerusalem Trail, another branch of the Long Trail off to your left. The Barton Trail on your right leads to Glen Ellen Lodge. Continue to follow the white blazes up to the ridge of General Stark Mountain and Stark's Nest, the upper station of the Mad River Glen Chair Lift. You can spend the night here during the summer when a Green Mountain Club Caretaker is in residence and if there is room. There is space for about ten to twelve people.

From Stark's Nest, the Long Trail follows the Fall Line Ski Trail, then enters the woods again. Follow the white blazes to Theron Dean Shelter, a log shelter with bunks for four to six people. (Theron Dean was an early member of the Green Mountain Club). Here the Long Trail bears right, crosses a level ridge, descends to Stark's Wall, passes through Chamberlain Glen, and finally reaches Route 17 (McCullough Turnpike) at Appalachian Gap. You can leave a car here, or arrange to have someone meet you.

For more information about the Long Trail, call the Green Mountain Club at (802) 223-3463. There is also an excellent book called *The Long Trail Guidebook*, available in most Vermont bookstores or through the Green Mountain Club in Montpelier. It describes the trail and gives valuable information about places to stay, what to expect, and some of the history of the trail.

CENTRAL VERMONT

Woodstock Walking Tour (89)

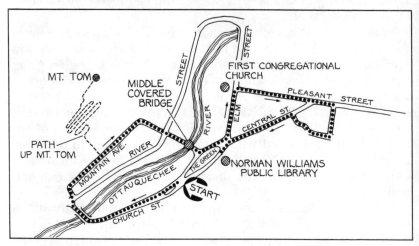

Directions: Woodstock is about three hours from Boston. Take I-93 north to I-89, and take exit 1 in Vermont. Turn left on Route 4, and drive west for about 14 miles to Woodstock. This walk begins at the Village Green.

Best Season: Late spring, summer, and fall, from about June 1st through October 31st.

Length: About 1½ miles.

Degree of Difficulty: Easy.

Highlights: You'll stroll through a picture-perfect New England village on this walk which starts at one of the most picturesque Greens in America and passes by stately old homes and charming shops.

Nestled in the foothills of the Green Mountains, Woodstock is considered to be one of the loveliest villages in America, its stately eighteenth- and nineteenth-century homes and its beautiful Green and charming shops reminders of an earlier time.

The first settler arrived in Woodstock in 1765, and twenty years later the village became the Shire Town, or seat, of Windsor County. As a result, business and professional people were attracted to Woodstock; they brought an established culture with them, and they built large and elegant homes. Shops and small industries grew up around the Green, including a silversmith's shop, a saddlery, a hatter's shop, a bakery, tailor, and blacksmith shop. There were also two printing shops, a jewelry store, a tannery, tin shop, cabinet-maker's store, and two schools. Two hotels and a courthouse were built. Lumber, wool, and cider-pressing mills grew up along the streams, and numerous industries, including pottery and cooperage, bookbinding, and basket making arose in the outlying districts. At one time five weekly newspapers competed with one another, and agriculture flourished. For years, Windsor County was the U.S. center for the Jersey cow.

Woodstock's peak as an industrial and population center passed in the mid-nineteenth century, but the picturesque village has continued to be a popular resort area both in summer and winter. This walk, nominated by Sam Merlo and Donald Wheeler, begins at the Woodstock Green and goes west along Church Street over the Ottauquechee River to Mountain Avenue. Turn right on Mountain, and then right again on Union Street. The Trailhead for a walk up Mt. Tom is off Mountain Avenue, and you may want to take this beautiful side trip. Follow Union Street through the Middle Covered Bridge, which was completed in 1969 and is the first authentic covered bridge built on a highway in New Hampshire or Vermont this century.

When you reach the Green again, turn left, and then make another left onto Elm Street. You'll pass the Woodstock Historical Society's Dana House, which was built in 1807. Inside you'll find a library, early nineteenth-century furnishings, old toys and dolls, photographs, and costumes. Where Elm meets Pleasant Street, you'll come to the First Congregational Church, which was built in 1808. The steeple bell (which cracked in 1974 and now stands on the south porch of the church) was cast by Paul Revere and family. Three other Revere bells still ring in Woodstock churches.

Walk down Pleasant Street to Bond Street and turn right, then right on Central Street. Just before you reach the Green again, on your left, you'll see the Norman Williams Public Library. Stop inside for a look at a marvelous collection of Japanese Art.

Back at the Green, nominator Sam Merlo suggests you pause for a moment to contemplate a bit of folklore. It seems that in 1818, a large crowd of some 10,000 people gathered here to witness the hanging of Samuel Godfrey, the accused killer of the state prison warden. Hangings drew crowds in those days!

SOUTHERN VERMONT

Silver Lake Loop (90)

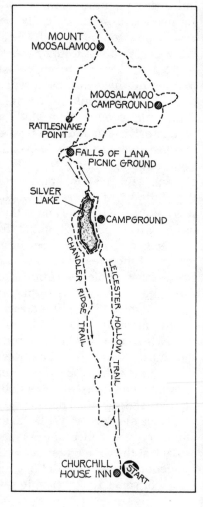

Directions: The walk begins at the Churchill House Inn, just west of the Brandon Gap. From Rutland, take Route 7 north to Brandon, and turn right on Route 73. Drive east on 73 to the inn, which will be on your left.

Best Season: Mid-May through fall.

Length: 10 miles round-trip; allow a full day and bring a picnic lunch.

Degree of Difficulty: Easy to moderate.

Highlights: A peaceful trail winds through the woods to a crystal clear lake which makes a great place for a picnic lunch.

The Churchill House Inn, where this walk begins, is part of a group called Country Inns Along the Trail, which enables visitors to participate in a variety of self-guided activities in combination with visits to some of the warm, friendly, historic country inns of Vermont. The concept, developed by the Churchill House Inn, allows hikers to walk along various trails at their own pace, including an 80-mile section of the popular Long Trail, and to stop at inns along the way.

This particular walk from the Churchill House Inn was nominated by Brenda Fizur. It makes a loop from the inn following the Leicester Hollow Trail to Silver Lake, then returning via the Chandler Ridge Trail. From Churchill House Inn, walk up the road, and make a left past the driveway into Leicester Hollow. Follow the trail along the stream; it crosses wonderful wooden bridges covered with moss. In spring, wildflowers add spots of color to the tree-shaded path. When you reach Silver Lake, you'll pass a campground and then you'll come to a picnic area. Stop for lunch and a swim before continuing around the lake to pick up the Chandler Ridge Trail on the other side and begin the return trip. At the intersection of the two trails there is a side trail leading to the Falls of Lana. This, too, makes a wonderful place for a picnic lunch.

The Chandler Ridge Trail is higher than the Leicester Hollow Trail and you'll have some very nice views on your return trip. Brenda says you can see the Green Mountains and beautiful Lake Dunmore in the distance. Chandler Ridge Trail connects with the Leicester Hollow Trail and from there, you can retrace your steps back to the inn.

This hike can be extended from the Falls of Lana by taking the Mt. Moosalamoo Trail past Rattlesnake Point to the Moosalamoo Campground and then returning to Lana Falls via the North Branch Trail. This will add about 8 miles to your walk, so you'll have to leave early in the morning or plan to camp at Moosalamoo or Silver Lake. Check in at the Churchill House Inn before you begin the walk for information on trail conditions and hiking times. Also, if you would like more information about Country Inns Along the Trail, you can write: Churchill House Inn, RD 3, Brandon, Vermont 05733, or call: (802) 247-3300.

SOUTHERN VERMONT

Lye Brook Waterfalls (91)

Directions: The Lye Brook Waterfalls are located in the Lye Brook Wilderness Area of the Green Mountain National Forest. To enter the wilderness you must have a permit which you can get at the Dis-

trict Ranger's office in the Cata-
mount National Bank Building in
Manchester Center (on Route 7).
To get to the Trailhead, take Routes
11 and 30 east from Manchester
Center to Glen Road. Turn onto
Glen Road, and keep straight once
you've gone over the first bridge
(Glen Road goes off to the left). Follow the road straight ahead for
about ½ mile to the parking area.

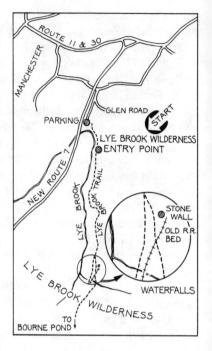

Best Season: Summer and fall.

Length: 4.6 miles round-trip. Nominator Pamela Boyd suggests you
pack a picnic lunch and plan to
spend the whole day.

Degree of Difficulty: Moderately
difficult; parts of the trail are steep,
and there are small streams to
cross; fallen logs and branches
may block the trail in some areas.

Highlights: This is a wonderfully scenic and peaceful walk in the
heart of the Lye Brook Wilderness.

The blue-blazed trail to Lye Brook Waterfalls begins at the bulle-
tin board in the parking area. As you start out, you'll come to a stream
on your right, and before long the trail begins to climb. You'll cross
over a couple of small streams and continue up until the trail makes
a wide turn to the right. Continue to climb (you can see the valley now,
spreading out below you on the right), and watch closely for a diag-
onal crossing of an old railroad bed. On your left you'll see the stone
wall which was part of the bed. At this point you have walked 2
miles. Turn right and follow the railroad bed for about ⅓ mile, carefully negotiating any logs or fallen branches that may block the path.

Almost out of nowhere it seems the falls appear, the cascading water filling the silent wilderness with a crashing sound. Continue along the trail, through a thicket of small spruce trees, to the gorge. Here you'll see the remains of an old railroad trestle which served to carry trainloads of logs over the stream on their way to sawmills down in the valley.

Spend as much time as you like near the waterfalls, enjoying the picturesque beauty of this protected wilderness area.

After your walk to the falls, drive back to Manchester Center, and head south on Route 7 to the town of Manchester, which has been a popular resort village for more than 100 years. It is a particularly elegant New England town, with beautiful historic buildings, a white-steepled church, and a picture-perfect Town Green—all nestled in the shadow of the tallest peak in the Taconic Mountain range, the 3,816-foot Mount Equinox. A toll road, Skyline Drive (usually closed from the end of October to May) winds through the trees to the summit, where you can enjoy wonderful views of the Green Mountains, the Berkshires in Massachusetts, and parts of New York State.

SOUTHERN VERMONT

Townshend Forest Trail (92)

Directions: The trail is located in Townshend State Forest in Windham County. From Brattleboro, take Route 30 through Newfane to Townshend. Turn left on State Park Road and follow signs; the trail is blazed in blue and the Trailhead is marked.

Best Season: June through September.

Length: About 3 miles round-trip.

Degree of Difficulty: Moderately difficult; from the campsite there is a vertical climb up 1,680 feet to the summit of Bald Mountain.

Highlights: Beautiful trees and flowers, interesting geologic formations, diverse wildlife, and lovely views are all part of this delightful walk.

"This walk can be an entire day's event," says nominator Nadia Tarlow. "First of all, the drive to get there is beautiful; then, once you're there you won't want to leave, and finally, there's a great place to swim and picnic after the walk."

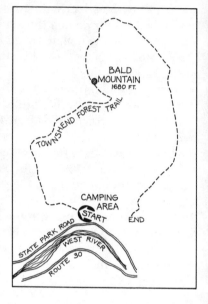

The drive to Townshend State Forest is, indeed, a beautiful one. Route 30 follows the West River, where you may see a kayaker or two, and you'll pass through the historic town of Newfane, known for its quintessential New England Town Square. When you get to Townshend, stop for a look at the Congregational Church. It was built in 1790 and is one of the most photographed churches in New England. Along the gravel road that leads to the campsite, you'll see Scott Covered Bridge, the longest single-span bridge of its type in Vermont. It was built in 1870 and spans 165.7 feet with a single horizontal timber. Today, covered bridges evoke nostalgia, and people drive for miles to see them. The techniques used to build them were adapted from barn construction, and they were covered, not to look pretty, but to protect the wood surfaces from changing weather conditions.

As you climb to the summit of the 1,680-foot-high Bald Mountain, you'll pass through groves of many different kinds of trees, including aspen, beech, black cherry, butternut, elm, birch, oak, maple, ash, and basswood. You'll see lots of evergreens too—hemlock, spruce, balsam fir, cedar, tamarack, and pine. At the top, views of the ski slopes on Mt. Bromley and Mt. Stratton await you to the west, and if it's a clear day, you'll be able to see Mt. Monadnock (3,186 feet) to the east in New Hampshire.

At the end of your walk Nadia suggests you drive over Townshend Dam to the Townshend Reservoir Recreation Area, where you can cool off with a nice swim or rent a boat. If you are taking this walk in May, you may want to get back on Route 30 and drive a few miles to the little village of Jamaica. The National Canoe and Kayak Championship Races are held here in May on the West River.

SOUTHERN VERMONT

Main Street, Windsor (93)

Directions: Located on the Connecticut River, Windsor is accessible from I-91 where it passes Vermont's Route 44. This walk begins on North Main Street at Elijah's Tavern, the "birthplace of Vermont," now called the Old Constitution House.

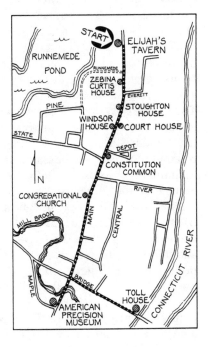

Best Season: Mid-May through mid-October.

Length: Allow at least half a day to explore Windsor.

Degree of Difficulty: Easy.

Highlights: This walk down Windsor's historic Main Street includes a look at the "birthplace of Vermont," numerous stately old eighteenth- and nineteenth-century homes, a fascinating machine and tool museum, and the Vermont State Craft Center at Windsor House.

On July 8, 1777, a group of delegates gathered in Elijah West's tavern and adopted a constitution for the "Free and Independent State of Vermont." In addition to giving the state a new name (the area had previously been known as *New Connecticut*), this constitution became the first in the country to outlaw slavery and guarantee universal male suffrage. Elijah's Tavern, thought to be the state's oldest building, dates from around 1774. It was relocated to its present site on North Main Street, where it now serves as a museum (open daily from mid-May through mid-October) called Old Constitution House. This walk down Windsor's Main Street, which begins at Elijah's Tavern, has been adapted from the book *Walking Tours of New England*, by Kenneth Winchester and David Dunbar.

From Elijah's Tavern, head south on Main Street, noting the beautiful homes and the variety of architecture. Past Runnemede Lane, you'll come to the Zebina Curtis House on your right. Built in 1796, this house was known as the "White House" when Senator Evarts, secretary of state for Rutherford B. Hayes, lived here.

Continue along Main Street, past Everett Lane, to the Stoughton House, one of Windsor's most elegant homes. Built in 1833, the house has had a somewhat stormy history (at least two of its previous owners ended in financial ruin), and gets its name from Edwin Stoughton, who was the U.S. Ambassador to Russia in 1877 and did not suffer from financial woes. Stoughton was responsible for turning the house (now a senior citizen home) into a showplace.

The Post Office on your left is the oldest continuously used Post Office/Federal Court House in the United States. It was designed by Amni Young. Across the street is Windsor House, where more than 250 craftspeople display and sell their crafts. Craft and preservation skills are offered here throughout the year. Once a grand hotel where presidents and royalty slept, Windsor House is still a vibrant, exciting place, alive today with the traditional skills of the area.

Just before you reach State Street, you'll pass Constitution Common, the original site of Elijah's Tavern. Here you can sit and rest for a while before continuing on down Main Street, past State and River streets, to the Old South Congregational Church. Built in 1798, you'll find the grave of Samuel Smith, the first boy born in Windsor, in the church burial ground. The earliest grave dates back to 1766.

Last on this tour of Windsor's Main Street is the American Precision Museum at the corner of Main and Maple. In the quiet, peaceful atmosphere of today's Windsor, it may be difficult to imagine that the town was once an industrial center, but in fact Windsor was the "cradle of the American machine tool industry." This museum, open from May 30th through mid-October, affords a fascinating glimpse into Windsor's role in the development of mass production.

On your return trip, take a walk downhill along Bridge Street to the Connecticut River. The building on your left is Toll House. It was built around 1797 to collect fares from people using the "longest covered bridge in America." The last toll (rates ranged from 2¢ for pedestrians to 20¢ for a four-horse carriage) was collected in 1943.

SOUTHERN VERMONT

Old Bennington (94)

Directions: Bennington is located on U.S. Route 7 in the southwest corner of Vermont, about 140 miles from Boston. Take U.S. 7 to Vermont's Route 9, which becomes Main Street in Bennington. Head west to Old Bennington, and park on West Main Street. The walk begins nearby at the Bennington Battle Monument, on the corner of Monument Avenue and Walloomsac Street.

Best Season: Early summer.

Length: Only about 2 miles; but there's lots to do and see in Bennington, so you may want to plan on at least half a day.

Degree of Difficulty: Easy.

Highlights: A chance to relive the historic Battle of Bennington and to pass by one of the greatest concentrations of early Georgian and Federal-style homes in all of Vermont.

On August 16, 1777, one of the fiercest battles of the American Revolution was fought at Bennington, Vermont, as 2,000 American militiamen routed the British and ended General Burgoyne's hopes of cutting New England off from the other colonies. The battle is considered "the turning point of the Revolution" by historians, for it revived the flagging spirits of the colonists and helped ensure an American victory two months later at the Battle of Saratoga. The Bennington Battle Monument, where this walk begins, is a 306-foot-high blue limestone obelisk. It was dedicated in 1891 to commemorate the historic battle. The monument is open daily from April to the end of October; an elevator takes visitors up to a gallery from which there are panoramic views of the countryside.

But Bennington is much more than a battle site. Nestled between the Taconic range to the west and the Green Mountains to the east, it is a charming New England town. This walk, nominated by Pat McCready, takes you past elegant old homes of the eighteenth and nineteenth centuries and into many other buildings of beauty and significance.

From the Battle Monument, walk down Monument Avenue, and note the variety of old homes on either side. Opposite Bank Street is one of the most impressive; a stately Georgian Colonial that was built for General David Robinson in 1795 so that he might live in a more elegant dwelling. The general's mother, the widow of Bennington pioneer Samuel Robinson, must have had a strong will, for she refused to move into the new house. It wasn't until after her death that the Robinson family moved in. The home remained in their possession until 1937. On the southern corner of Bank and Main streets stands the Old Academy, which was built in 1821 as a school. Later it was used as a library and prayer meeting room. The Parson Dewey Home toward the southern end of Monument Avenue is thought to be one of the oldest frame dwellings in Vermont. The Reverend Jedediah

Dewey, the first minister of the First Meeting House, built the home himself in 1763.

When you reach Elm Street, retrace your steps back up Monument Avenue to Main Street and turn right for a visit to the Old First Church and the adjacent Old Burying Ground, where Robert Frost is buried. The epitaph on his headstone reads: "I had a lover's quarrel with the world." Among others buried here are five Vermont governors, and there is a common tombstone honoring soldiers who died in the Battle of Bennington.

From the Old First Church, continue east on Main Street to the Bennington Museum, where you can see the oldest American flag in existence; it flew during the Battle of Bennington. The museum houses an outstanding collection of American paintings, sculpture, silver, and furniture, and more than thirty paintings by Grandma Moses are displayed in a re-creation of the schoolhouse the beloved painter of primitives once attended. The museum is open daily from 9 a.m. to 5 p.m., from March 1 to November 30 (except Thanksgiving Day).

After your visit to the museum, retrace your steps down Main Street, and cross Monument Avenue to West Main Street. On the corner of Main and Monument, you'll see the Walloomsac Inn, which may be the oldest in Vermont. It was built around 1766 and has been in continuous operation ever since. Prisoners from the Battle of Bennington were fed from the inn's kitchen, and later, after the Revolution, it became an important stage stop. The inn has welcomed many illustrious guests, including Thomas Jefferson, James Madison, and Rutherford B. Hayes.

NORTHERN VERMONT

Stowe Recreation Path (95)

Directions: Take I-89 to Waterbury. Go north on Route 100 to Stowe Village. The walk starts behind the white church on Main Street.

Best Season: Each season has its own special charm, but nominator Anne Lusk likes fall the best.

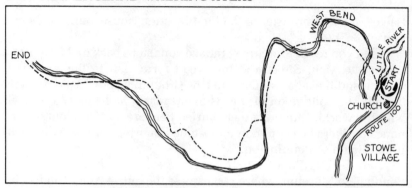

Length: Two hours round-trip for the 2.7-mile part of the path, and two hours round-trip for the 2.6-mile extension (not completed as of this writing).

Degree of Difficulty: Easy; the path is paved and relatively flat.

Highlights: A picturesque path built and beloved by the towns-people and friends of Stowe which offers views of Mt. Mansfield, Vermont's tallest mountain, and proximity to the village's charming architecture.

"This path is a model in the state," says Anne Lusk, who told us about it, "not only because of its beauty, but also because the towns-people and friends of Stowe built it. It is one of Stowe's best-shared secrets." And Anne has noticed something particularly special about the path. "Stowe has sidewalks where local people and tourists pass one another all the time. They may smile faintly, but they rarely speak. Yet those same people, when walking on the Recreation Path not only smile openly, they share enthusiastic friendly exchanges. It's a different world on the path."

The eight-foot-wide paved path begins behind the Greek Revival Community Church on Main Street. The first section crosses twenty-seven different properties, including one farm, all donated by towns-people through deeds of easement. A list of the contributors who helped make the path a reality can be seen on the "Donor Sign" at the beginning of the walk. "Stowe's pride in this path," Anne says, "has been evident not only by the town's willingness to fund and build it, but also by its eagerness to share it with visitors and by its desire to tell others how they, too, can build a path or 'greenway.'"

Anne herself has written a pamphlet called *How to Build a Path in Your Community*. It is available at the Selectmen's Office, Akeley Memorial Building, on Main Street.

The first bridge you will cross on your walk curves over the Little River and leads to a field where you can see the backs of the buildings on Main Street and the New England picture-postcard homes of Maple Street. As you head for the second bridge, the path bends around ancient maple, spruce, and elm trees because no one wanted to disturb these magnificent old trees when the path was built. A break in the trees to the right reveals a stand of 100-year-old white pines which guard the cemetery.

The path now goes over another bridge and through a glen to the first farm, the fields bordered by the house and barns and framed by the hills. Continue on to the third bridge, where the terrain changes from open fields to woodland, with wildflowers everywhere in spring and rich green ferns in summer. Nearby, Anne says, there's the "best swimming hole, with a rope in a branch marking the spot."

Stowe's path allows its visitors the opportunity to walk or cross-country ski to lodges, dining, and recreation without ever needing a car. After the fourth bridge, there is access to a few of Stowe's much-heralded restaurants. Stop for breakfast, a coffee break, a patio lunch, or a special dinner, depending on the time of day.

Once refreshed, pick up the path, and walk to the fifth and sixth bridges where the land opens up again, this time to views of Mt. Mansfield. The path ends at the beginning of the proposed new extension. "Legend has it," Anne explains, "that a child, overly eager to ride his bike on the path, followed the macadam machine too closely, and the heat of the tar burst his tire. A description of the extension will be available when the pavement has cooled."

NORTHERN VERMONT

Camel's Hump (96)

Directions: Camel's Hump is located in Camel's Hump State Park, which is part of the larger Camel's Hump Forest Reserve. From Montpelier, take I-89 north and follow signs.

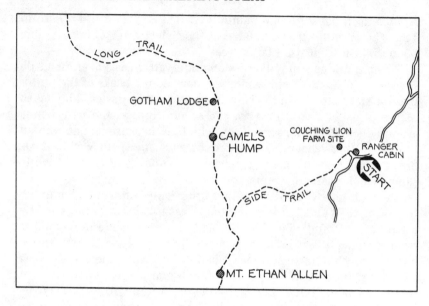

Best Season: Spring through fall.

Length: Trails to the summit of Camel's Hump vary in length; the Long Trail climbs to the summit in just under 10 miles from the Montclair Glen Lodge.

Degree of Difficulty: Moderate to difficult.

Highlights: The rewards of this walk are wonderful vistas of mountains in New York, New Hampshire, Vermont, and Canada, as well as a spectacular view of almost all of Lake Champlain.

This 4,083-foot mountain peak (tied with Mt. Ellen as the third highest in Vermont) is not only the most popular with hikers, it is also the most recognizable. The Waubanaukee Indians called it the "saddle mountain," and later explorers with Samuel de Champlain thought it resembled a sleeping lion and called it "le lion couchant," which was sloppily translated as "The Couching Lion." In 1798, the name *Camel's Rump* first appeared on a map of the area; this was amended to *Camel's Hump* in 1830, and since then the name has not changed.

In 1911, 1,000 acres, including the summit of Camel's Hump, were conveyed to the state of Vermont by Colonel Joseph Battell, who specified that the forest was "to be preserved in a primeval state." Today the state owns more than 19,000 acres, and Camel's Hump remains the only undeveloped high peak in Vermont. In 1968, it became a Registered National Landmark, and despite the fact that more than 10,000 people enjoy hiking on Camel's Hump each year, the Vermont Agency of Development and Community Affairs has made a promise to this mountain—a promise "that the only changes it would undergo are Spring, Summer, Fall and Winter." Everyone who is involved with Camel's Hump is committed to this promise. Be careful when you make your visit that you don't violate the promise. Plants above treeline are especially vulnerable to human intrusion. The summit of Camel's Hump supports the second-largest area of alpine tundra in Vermont. This vegetation is irreplaceable. *Stay on the trails.*

There are several routes to the summit of this mountain, including the Long Trail, which runs through the Camel's Hump Forest Reserve and over the "Hump." It is suggested that you stop by the Couching Lion Farm Ranger Station near the base of the mountain, where state rangers or members of the Green Mountain Club can explain the ecology of the area and direct you to the least traveled route. You can also stop by the Camel's Hump View Inn in Moretown, where nominators Wilma and Jerry Maynard will describe their favorite hikes in the reserve and may even join you for a walk. (Heading north on I-89 from Montpelier, take 100B south to Moretown.)

Moretown is one of several small village centers within the reserve. All have maintained their rural charm, and you may want to allow some time to savor their picturesque valleys and open meadows, dotted here and there with white farmhouses and cows grazing on the hillsides. From the open valleys you'll have views of the surrounding mountains, including Camel's Hump.

NORTHERN VERMONT

Bayley Hazen Road to Greensboro (97)

Directions: This walk begins at the Presbyterian Church in East Craftsbury, a little village east of Route 14 in Vermont's "Northeast Kingdom." From Montpelier, take Route 2 east to Route 14, and drive north through some of the most scenic countryside in Vermont, for about 30 miles. Watch for signs to East Craftsbury on your right.

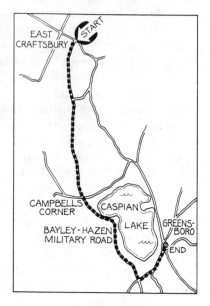

Best Season: May or September.

Length: 7 miles one way. Allow about two and a half hours, and double it if you plan to walk back. Often people who take this walk leave a car in Greensboro, and drive back to East Craftsbury.

Degree of Difficulty: Moderate.

Highlights: This is a walk back in time to Vermont's historic and agricultural past.

"Some of the special things about this walk," says nominator Natalie Kinsey-Warnock, "are the wide variety of road surfaces and terrain and the feeling of being taken back through Vermont's historic and agricultural past. The walk begins in a small Vermont village, travels through woods and abandoned farmland, and ends at another small village that is steeped in Vermont flavor."

Before actually starting out on the walk, most people like to pay a visit to the Scottish Woollen Shop in East Craftsbury. Owned by a British couple, the Godslands, this shop is the only one in the United States which has true Scottish woolens. Many people also like to stop in at the library, which used to be the general store.

A right turn past the library leads to the Bayley-Hazen Road, an old military road built by Col. Moses Hazen for the purpose of invading Montreal! Natalie says the first few miles along this old road are especially lovely in spring and fall when the leaves of the maple trees form a canopy over the road. Wildflowers are everywhere, and you'll see some evidence of old farms in the stone walls and apple trees hidden in the woods. "Except for the birdsong," Natalie says, "everything is still."

After a while, you'll come to a four-way dirt intersection where you'll get your first glimpse of Caspian Lake. Natalie suggests you stop here for a picnic lunch or walk to the nearby cemetery for a look at the epitaphs, many of them written for Natalie's own ancestors.

A few more miles of walking will take you into the village of Greensboro, where everyone loves to dawdle in Willey's Store. "It has *everything*," Natalie says, "from axe handles to cheese, from snowshoes to socks. We often celebrate the end of our walk here with an ice cream, or we go down to Caspian Lake for a swim. It's one of the most beautiful lakes in Vermont, and a wonderful place for swimming and windsurfing, too, as there is almost always some wind here."

NORTHERN VERMONT

The Lake Loop (98)

Directions: This walk is located in the village of Craftsbury Common, in Vermont's "Northeast Kingdom." From Montpelier (I-89, exit 8), take Route 2 east to Route 14 north, and drive for about 30 miles to Craftsbury Common. Continue north from the Common, for another 2½ miles. The walk starts at the Craftsbury Sports and Learning Center.

Best Season: May.

Length: 7.2 miles round-trip. Allow two to three hours.

Degree of Difficulty: Moderate.

Highlights: This beautiful loop walk around Lake Hosmer follows a rolling, twisting dirt road into the forest, over open meadows, and past immaculate farms and charming old farmhouses.

John Brodhead of the Craftsbury Sports Center nominated this walk and sent us a wonderful personal description of the day he first saw it up close:

"One morning early in May, I was sitting in my office at the Craftsbury Sports Center grumbling to myself about running injuries which had recently grounded me. A friend popped in and cheerfully asked if I wanted to walk the Lake Loop. Now, a runner could do this 7.2-mile walk in forty-five minutes. The prospect of walking for two hours or more over a distance that I had run probably a hundred times seemed tedious, but in my present condition, the options were limited. I laced up my Rockports and we were out the door and striding down the road in no time.

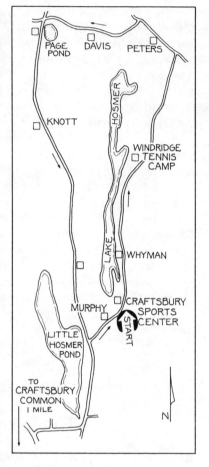

"The contrasts between running the Lake Loop and walking it immediately began to impress me. There was no special clothing to change into and no warmup or stretching to perform. My calf muscles, subject to chronic strain from running, were entirely free from stress, even at the most vigorous walking pace. Traveling at one-third my accustomed rate over this familiar route opened my eyes to an entirely different scene. We stopped occasionally to track down the source of a bird call or examine the flower structure of a wild member of the mustard family.

"May is a wonderful month to walk in Craftsbury. Spring, which arrives late here, is at its peak. Traffic is virtually nonexistent—one car in two hours. The Sports Center, a year-round 'campus' overlooking Lake Hosmer, is the start and finish of the Lake Loop. From the dining hall porch there is a view down the fjordlike lake, with its steep forested sides and deep clear waters. The route runs counterclockwise around the lake and dips and climbs seven moderate-size hills. A mosaic of hardwoods, soft woods, and open meadows lines the narrow road. Much of the way, sugar maples arch over completely, giving welcome shade on even the hottest days. In Vermont's "Northeast Kingdom," development and subdivision are remarkably scant. With few exceptions, the largely unaltered farmsteads have been in the same family for generations.

"A half mile north of the Center, Stacy Whyman is sitting on his slightly sagging porch, resting after a strenuous bout of cutting an overgrown lawn. His 150-year-old home has the air of an old country farmhouse. As we pass by, Stacy calls out 'Hello!'

"The road dips now, down to a cedar swamp and fir forest where we hear a subtle change in the chorus of bird calls. The calls of red starts and rose-breasted grosbeaks, who had shouted their territorial insults in the more open areas, are replaced by the discreet taunts of the bay-breasted and Cape May warblers.

"Windridge Tennis Camp is not in session until the middle of June; a brief side trip of about 100 yards to a grassy hilltop here offers panoramic vistas of the nearby Lowell Range to the west.

"Two and a half miles, a left turn, and a short climb takes us to Bill Peters' place. Bill is the quintessential 'Real Vermonter,' gruff on the exterior, but one of the finest people around to those who know him. His dog is a no-nonsense German shepherd, perhaps with a slight chip on his shoulder. Somewhere he lost his tail. Most of the time, he is restrained on a rope, but not always. Bill says, 'He only goes after bikers or runners. Just walk slowly and he won't bother you.' We pass by, and the shepherd pretends to sleep.

"Doctor Davis lives in the green farmhouse with big porches all around it, across from his Morgan Horse Farm. This is the three-and-a-half-mile mark. The doctor has retired from delivering babies and now tends his flock of geese and a few show horses. At Page Pond Four Corners, turn left and start the homeward leg. The 20-acre pond is a wonderful habitat for all manner of birdlife. As you approach Blue Gate Farm, the four-and-a-half-mile mark, look for hoofprints in the sandy road. The nearby fence is not very high, and frisky ponies regularly break loose for a gambol down the road. Pauline Knott resides here. She is renowned for her temper with trespassers and for her friendly demeanor with walkers who stay on the road.

"After another mile and a half, the trail begins a long descent. On the left is a well-manicured summer home with splendid views to the south overlooking Little Hosmer Pond. The pastureland beyond makes a gradual rise to Craftsbury Common; cows dot the distant meadows, and a church steeple is just visible.

"We make our last left, and climb to the seven-mile mark where there is a view of the Green Mountains to the southwest. Camel's Hump and Mount Mansfield, visible over the tops of intervening lesser mountains, glisten with late snow patches near their summits. John Murphy, recently retired from banking, is master of this view. His renovated farmhouse and gentleman farm bear the marks of a considerable investment of time and money. He has found the ideal place to live out the rest of his days in peace and contemplation.

"A few more steps and we are back at the Center, having made a complete circle of the lake, unseen but pervasive."

NORTHERN VERMONT

Nichols Ledge (99)

Directions: This walk begins at the Kahagon Inn in Hardwick, which is located off the junction of Routes 14 and 15 in Vermont's "Northeast Kingdom." From Hardwick, follow Route 14 south and take the first dirt road (Mackville Road) on your left to Kahagon Inn.

Best Season: Fall for the foliage; spring for wildflowers.

Length: 3 miles. Allow about one hour.

Degree of Difficulty: Moderately difficult; the walk is short, but the hill is steep in some places. There is one muddy section in the woods, and you need to be careful on the ledge.

Highlights: Breathtaking views and a real wilderness feeling are the rewards of this secluded, scenic walk.

This walk begins at the dirt road on the right, below Kahagon Inn. After about 1 mile, the road levels off, and the trail to the cliff leads off to the right. You'll walk through the woods at first, where you'll have an opportunity to see some very special wildflowers and to hear the call of a variety of birds. Peregrine falcons have nested on the cliff for the past couple of years, and nominator Natalie Kinsey-Warnock has heard loons calling from Nichols Pond. "Their eerie, mournful cry carries on the wind that always seems to blow from the mountains to the west," she explains. She goes on to say, "Almost every time I have hiked up to the ledge, I have watched hawks (red-tailed, red-shouldered, broad-winged, and marsh) soar by on the updrafts. I think if I were a bird, I would choose to live here, because one does get the urge to fly when standing on this wild, granite eyrie."

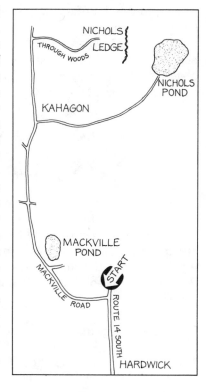

From the woods, the trail climbs steeply for about ½ mile to the top of Nichols Ledge, the site of an old granite quarry. A pile of the old, cut granite blocks can be seen at the foot of the cliff (be careful if you are adventurous enough to lean out over the ledge to see them!). This short walk has a wonderful wilderness feeling to it, and the granite ledge evokes Vermont's past, when this hard volcanic rock was a force in the industry of the "Granite State." "The stone is symbolic of our state," Natalie says, "and of the strong, independent people who live here."

Nichols Ledge is a "very special place" to Natalie, who was married here twelve years ago. "I chose the ledge for my wedding because of its unique beauty," she says. "The view from the cliffs is spectacular, looking west across the spine of the Green Mountains and on to the Adirondacks in New York. The cliff overlooks three large secluded ponds and a vast section of woods made up mostly of maple trees. The maples are breathtaking when seen in their autumnal array of colors. If it weren't for two farms you can see in the far distance, you could almost forget that other humans exist.''

NORTHERN VERMONT

Main Street, St. Johnsbury (100)

Directions: St. Johnsbury is located in Vermont's "Northeast Kingdom," at the intersection of I-91 and I-93, about 160 miles from Boston. This walk begins at the St. Johnsbury Academy at the south end of Main Street.

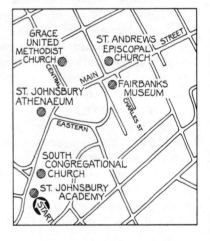

Best Season: Spring through fall.

Length: Allow about one hour for the walk itself, but allow a whole day if you plan to stop at the museums along the way.

Degree of Difficulty: Easy.

Highlights: This walk along St. Johnsbury's Main Street encompasses several churches, numerous homes of architectural significance, an outstanding art gallery at the Saint Johnsbury's Athenaeum, and a visit to the Fairbanks Museum of Natural History.

This walk was created by Dr. Norman Atwood, a St. Johnsbury native with a deep appreciation for Victorian architecture, who prepared the walk for the Bicentennial St. Johnsbury House Foundation. It begins at Brantview, a Queen Anne–style chateau which was finished in 1885 for William P. Fairbanks, a nephew of Thaddeus

Fairbanks, the inventor of a platform scale for weighing hemp that virtually began St. Johnsbury's industrial history. The Fairbanks Weighing Division is still making scales just outside St. Johnsbury. Today Brantview is a dormitory for the St. Johnsbury Academy. Walking north on Main Street, you'll come to the South Congregational Church, which was built in 1852. Its high white spire and elegant simplicity are typical of many beautiful churches in New England. The Emerson Hall House at 20 Main Street is, according to Dr. Atwood, "a great house indeed." Built in 1872, it has a high mansard roof, a beautiful porch, and wonderful decorative details.

The St. Johnsbury Athenaeum is next on the tour, and you will certainly want to spend some time in this beautiful old building which houses an extensive collection of books and an outstanding old art gallery with an exhibit that includes Albert Bierstadt's "Domes of Yosemite." As you leave the Athenaeum to continue your walk up Main Street, be sure to note the old street clock at Main and Eastern Avenue. "It once told time in New York City's Grand Central Station," Dr. Atwood says. "Since 1910, it has told time, from time to time, here."

The Fairbanks Block at 35 Main Street was built by Lambert Packard in 1890. This neo-Romanesque building was once a store and now serves as an office for the St. Johnsbury Trucking Company. When you reach Central Street, turn left and walk to the Grace United Methodist Church, which is worth a visit mainly because of the Bethlehem window in the south wall; it was created by Louis Comfort Tiffany. Back on Main Street again, another church, St. Andrews Episcopal Church (56 Main), has a charming interior with hammer beam arches, an old organ, and a St. Andrew portrait window in the apse. The North Congregational Church at 78 Main Street, a "great New England Victorian Church," contains cherry woodwork, a stately organ, and elaborate pulpit furniture.

Walk now to the corner of Main and Charles streets for a visit to the Fairbanks Museum of Natural History. This building was built in 1896 by Lambert Packard from designs by H. H. Richardson for several libraries in Massachusetts. "Note the great wagon vault in the high central room," says Dr. Atwood, "the carvings in the fireplaces, the huge bird collection, the oriental and oceanic collections, the clocks, and northern Vermont memorabilia. There is a planetarium as well; a statuary group over a window in the facade shows

Science and her supporters—a lion and a guardian crane. The crane is shown with one foot lifted, and it is holding a little stone. If the crane should drowse, it would drop the stone on its other foot and awaken. Bronze lions on either side of the entrance test the courage of children about to enter the museum. This building, too, is a major achievement in New England architecture."

The big North Church Manse at 85 Main Street is notable for its use of Stick style, and its handsome front doors. You can see the Summer Street School, with its mansard-roofed bell tower, by looking left down the Common from Main Street. Continuing your walk, you'll note the Brooks House at 89 Main Street, a blend of Italianate and neo-Gothic styles, and the C. H. Stevens House at 110 Main Street. This elegant home by Lambert Packard has a Queen Anne–style corner tower, an eyebrow window in the roof, and beautiful interiors. The floor plan of the Federal-style Ephraim Paddock House at 115 Main Street was adapted from plans by Charles Bulfinch. Finally, the Estabrooks House at 123 Main Street, also by Lambert Packard, is, according to Dr. Atwood, "a photographer's dream, with a full catalogue of Queen Anne features: eyebrow window, stained glass, tower, pavilioned porch, arabesques in pressed metal in the gable, a small upstairs porch on brackets, and cast-iron frill on the rooftop.

On Mt. Pleasant Street at the north end of Main Street is a wooden octagonal house with a hidden chamber and a history of "ghosts." It has bracketed eaves in the Italianate manner of 1863. Halfway down Eastern Avenue from Main Street is another splendid octagonal house with a central circular stair and both a barn and an office building that are octagons. The house and office are brick with stone lintels. Italianate bracketed eaves and an air of magnificence exemplify the style.

BEST WALK NOMINATION FORM

(Please use additional paper when necessary)

Type and name of walk: _____

Region: _____

How to get there from the highway: _____

_____

Why selected: _____

Degree of difficulty: (Easy, moderate, moderately difficult, difficult, very difficult) Why? _____

Best time of year to go:_____

Description of walk (please include map and black-and-white photo if possible) _____

Physical environment: _____

Points of interest along the route (including interesting people you might meet along the way). Please include a statement of fifty words or more and/or a brochure: _____

_____

Walking time and distance: _____

Any warnings or hazards? _____

Personal statement: Your experiences during the walk (please include a statement of fifty words or more): _____

_____

Additional comments or information: _____

_____

The information I have provided is true to the best of my knowledge. I understand and agree that this information and materials become the property of Walking World, *to be used at its discretion. I also agree that my name can be used in connection with the publication of the walk.*

_____

(Signature)

(Please print): Name: _____

Address: _____

Telephone: _____

Please send to: *Walking World*
P.O. Box K, Gracie Station
New York, NY 10028

ABOUT THE AUTHORS

Gary Yanker has been dubbed walking's foremost authority in America, Europe, and Japan by *USA Today, The New York Times*, NBC News, Japan's *Asahi Shinhum* and Germany's *Frankfurter Allgemeine*, among others. His six previous bestselling walking books and tapes, including *The Complete Book of Exercisewalking* and *Walking Workouts*, have sold over 500 million copies worldwide. He has served as the walking editor for both *American Health* and *Prevention* magazines and helped found Walking World.

Carol D. Tarlow is a former senior editor of Reader's Digest Condensed Books. She is co-author, with Gary Yanker, of *America's Greatest Walks*. She heads her own writing and editing business in California.